THE MANSION
ACROSS THE STREET

THE MANSION ACROSS THE STREET

Abundantly Beyond All That We Think or Ask

ROSE ANNE DANIELS

WESTBOW
PRESS®
A DIVISION OF THOMAS NELSON
& ZONDERVAN

WestBow Press books may be ordered through booksellers or by contacting:

WestBow Press
A Division of Thomas Nelson & Zondervan
1663 Liberty Drive
Bloomington, IN 47403
www.westbowpress.com
1 (866) 928-1240

Because of the dynamic nature of the Internet, any web addresses or links contained in this book may have changed since publication and may no longer be valid. The views expressed in this work are solely those of the author and do not necessarily reflect the views of the publisher, and the publisher hereby disclaims any responsibility for them.

Any people depicted in stock imagery provided by Getty Images are models, and such images are being used for illustrative purposes only. Certain stock imagery © Getty Images.

Scripture taken from the NEW AMERICAN STANDARD BIBLE®, Copyright © 1960,1962,1963,1968,1971,1972,1973,1975,1977,1995 by The Lockman Foundation. Used by permission. www.Lockman.org

ISBN: 978-1-9736-7852-6 (sc)
ISBN: 978-1-9736-7851-9 (hc)
ISBN: 978-1-9736-7853-3 (e)

Library of Congress Control Number: 2019917281

Print information available on the last page.

WestBow Press rev. date: 11/07/2019

This book is dedicated to all who find themselves tight-lipped and desperate. My fondest hope is that you may find a kind listener who can also tell you truth. May you take action when it is needed and find the hope we all need to survive. To all those who have been such a listener, I am greatly in debt.

CONTENTS

INTRODUCTION

WHEN I WAS IN MY EARLY TWENTIES, I WAS faced with managing what was finally diagnosed as bipolar disorder. I was both devastated at the pronouncement and determined I would quickly be back to "normal." What I wanted most was to throw away the needed medicine, return to my whirlwind life, and enjoy my early-morning run without feeling drugged. I was the mother of two small children, and there wasn't time in my schedule for illness.

I was working as a registered nurse on a medical floor, and my doctor had me sit down one day while he explained that dealing with my illness was a lot like dealing with diabetes. He had my attention.

He asked me if I understood the delicate balance required by diabetics between medication and lifestyle, and indeed I did. He then went on to explain that I could either manage my illness with medication and a balanced lifestyle, or I could lose my eyesight or my limbs, suffer irreversible kidney damage, and possibly lose my life. Well, I had seen all of those consequences of diabetes not well managed. The word *picture* was just what I needed to jolt me into reality.

I'd like to say that I wised up right away. Certainly, that was my intention. As it was, my life took one devastating turn after another before a painfully slow climb out of the depths transpired.

Slowly, I came to understand the nature of adversity.

Over the years, I came to not only appreciate but to marvel at God's overwhelming abundance in the face of adversity. I came to appreciate the protective hand of the Almighty in giving me limits. Forced to draw apart from the crowd because of an illness I didn't choose, I learned to listen to the still, small voice from within. I came to understand that no detail of my life had escaped His almighty hand, and I came to appreciate the unique creation I was, forged upon the anvil of struggle.

I write this in hopes that others will come to know this guiding hand of grace and to take the needed leap of faith whenever life seems to offer no more possibilities.

> I waited patiently for the Lord;
> And He inclined to me and heard my cry.
> He brought me up out of the pit of
> destruction, out of the miry clay,
> And He set my feet upon a rock making my
> footsteps firm.
> He put a new song in my mouth, a song of
> praise to our God;
> Many will see and fear
> And will trust in the Lord. (Psalm 40:1–3)

CHAPTER 1

DREAMS CAN COME TRUE

"Have you ever had shock therapy?"

The question surprised me. The small, frail lady in front of me had apparently mused over our last conversation for some time prior to this moment.

"Yes," I replied, "but only over a two-week period. I'm not certain I would recommend it."

There was a long pause and a somewhat downcast appearance on the face of this person I had come to love. Two weeks prior, I had shared with her that I had bipolar disorder, after learning that she suffered from the same illness. We had engaged in small talk that was nothing of a substantial nature.

She asked me if I had ever been hospitalized with my condition, and I simply replied, "Too many times to recall. I stopped counting after twenty."

I sensed that she did not want to continue the conversation beyond that point, so we ended our chat. But apparently this dear lady had mused over our talk for quite a while before fate brought us together again.

She was perhaps fifteen years my senior. With somber eyes and a serious tone, she finally spoke. "I had it over four to five years."

I felt as though I had been punched in my midsection.

I had known this lady to be a meek and precious soul who never complained. Because I had written my story, I offered her one of my books. She quietly replied that she was unable to concentrate long enough to read.

Collecting myself, I solemnly inquired, "Where were you at the time?"

She mentioned a state psychiatric facility that is no longer in operation. I recognized the name and shuddered at the thought that this kind person had endured so much. Bit by bit, she told me the rest of her story.

She was in her late teens when the manic monster first appeared. It had eventually reduced her to a state inpatient involuntary commitment that lasted several years. Upon her eventual release, she met and married a soldier. Theirs was a rock-solid marriage that lasted the tribulations of the turbulent years that followed. He knew her history before the marriage. For her part, she was too shy to talk much at all when they first met. Yet he pursued her with abandon. Together, they endured the ups and downs of the bipolar affliction, several miscarriages, and her diagnosis of cancer. He was her best friend and vice versa. Although she was unable to return to paid employment, she had been his faithful partner while he worked to support them both. Never again was she committed.

We agreed on these certainties: Dreams can come true. We serve the God of the impossible. Suffering in this life is inevitable, but so is the joy that Jesus Christ can bring.

> Now to Him who is able to do far more abundantly beyond all that we ask or think, according to the power that works within us, to Him *be* the glory in the church and in Christ Jesus to all generations forever and ever. Amen. (Ephesians 3:20–21)

The phrase "abundantly beyond all that we ask or think" always conjures up the image of a mansion. I don't know how others would depict a mansion; there is only one picture from my childhood that comes to mind. I have seen this stately house not only in my youth but also in a vivid dream. It was to be my home, and I was to find the path that would lead to the grace and the undeserved riches it represented.

CHAPTER 2

THE MANSION

IT STOOD IN CONTRAST TO EVERY OTHER house in the neighborhood. A Southern brick colonial mansion with white pillars, it was built with slave labor in the 1840s. It later became a part of the Underground Railroad. A white icehouse behind the structure was used to hide slaves escaping to freedom in the North. I was awed at the appearance of the house, its extensive, beautifully landscaped grounds, and the history lesson it represented. My family lived in a modest dwelling across the street. In fact, all the dwellings across the street were meek by comparison. The only word my young vocabulary could fathom for this historic manor was *grand*.

I came to know, at the age of ten, that this house was owned by a medical doctor. I later learned that he had experienced tragedy in his life and used his skills and experience to benefit others. As a patient in his clinic, I learned that a quick wit and a ready smile greeted patients every day. He often clapped a patient on the back and told a good joke before he started the exam. At Christmastime, he sent poinsettias as well as his usual warm greetings to all his neighbors. We were on the receiving end of all this generosity.

Both sides of my family had long been farmers of simple means and were rather quick to judge anyone for affluence. Since we had recently sold the farm in exchange for small-town life, the decision as to which house to buy was certainly influenced by the house across the street. But after learning the owner was a doctor who was kind and generous, the judgments about those with wealth were rarely spoken. While curiosity and fascinations were certainly piqued, rarely was more than a telling gruff of envy muttered out loud by those of us looking on. Could it have been that we needed a neighbor who made house calls, as he frequently did?

My elder brother was asked if he would like a job tending the grounds of our honorable neighbors. He was quick to jump at the chance, and it seemed to me he took great pride in doing his work. After all, when cars slowed down to take in the sight, were they not taking in his careful tending? As for me, I envied the fact that he had been given such an honor. Eventually I would choose a career that was largely influenced by this neighbor's presence.

Except for the warmth of Christmas greetings, the occasional emergency when he came to our house, and the necessary clinic visits that my family made, we really saw little of this doctor and his family. They were private people. What my mother most wanted, I deduced, was a tour of the house. This was not granted until several years later, after our doctor retired from practice and sold the house to another family. Eventually, the new tenants invited my mother over to visit and take a tour. I tagged along for the long-awaited event. What surprised me most was that there were several rooms in the interior that were still in need of renovation. I had expected every room to be a grand ballroom, exquisitely and expensively furnished, but what I saw were modest living quarters and rooms yet unfinished. At some point, it became apparent to me that the owners of this mansion had preserved and restored history as a service to the community, much as they served the community in every other way.

After my brother, I was expected to have a paying job. I believe what I wanted most was to share the dignity he had acquired by being the caretaker of the mansion. Initially, this was simply not to be. But I would eventually find my way to a place of honor, influenced by our family doctor.

My first paying job at the age of fourteen was detasseling corn. It was hot, muddy work done in the heat of July. Walking seemingly endless rows of corn, a young crew would bend the overhead stalks to remove every other tassel. The Missouri River basin could not be counted on to produce a crop each year due to the danger of flooding. But the rich basin soil could yield hybrid seed, a high-paying crop in the years the corn survived. The local teenagers provided cheap labor, although my closest friends had parents who refused to let their daughters do such work. I had no such restrictions. The five o'clock in the morning trip to the fields was followed by a lonely row of towering corn that cut my skin and soaked me with dew until the sun came out. Then the noon ninety-eight-degree heat would dry, bake, and blister any skin left vulnerable. We were rewarded with minimum wage, although the crew boss often gave us an extra half hour of paid time out of sympathy.

I only submitted to this education for a couple of summers. It didn't take me long to find other work.

Next I became a busgirl at a local restaurant. The fine establishment was the nicest eatery in town. The busiest day was Sunday, when families would show up after church or afternoon dress parade at the local military academy. The owner hired only boys to bus tables for the most part; I was one of only two females hired for the job. I frequently endured jeers from my male coworkers and a pay scale that always put me at the bottom. I usually worked at the soda fountain, where I served the beverages and desserts, and I carried trays of dishes until my arms were tired. I frequently came home splattered with food and questionable proposals.

I learned from this experience. Still, it didn't take me long to find other work.

I finally became a nurse's aide at the local hospital. I was most honored to be working with women I admired and longed to emulate. At last, I felt I had found a place where I was needed and would be rewarded for my contributions. I was thrilled to be part of something noble as it seemed that I was finally working in a way that fulfilled my deepest needs and served my community. It was a bit like having a small job at the mansion. While I couldn't tend the groundwork, still I had learned how to tend. I had not an inkling of how God intended to use this desire in His master plan.

CHAPTER 3

WHAT I SEE FROM MY PORCH

SACRIFICIAL GIVING WAS DONE ON MY SIDE of the street. But this rather reluctant generosity was usually performed to relieve feelings of guilt rather than as an expression of joy of service. It was much like the obligatory bill in the church's collection plate accompanied by the sigh of the giver that I frequently witnessed. Money was a constant topic of discussion, and while we were all well fed and did not lack any basics, I heard discontent rather than gratitude on a regular basis. If our resources were indeed limited, I feared the God I served must not be listening. I took the task upon myself to pray daily for the requirements I clearly saw, and while my circumstances had changed, those of others had not.

First on my list was the need for my parents to be happy. They seemed brokenhearted in their daily lives, and I felt if that could just be changed, my life would be better also. We had a rather large family. My dad farmed and worked a full-time job. My mother battled depression and what I now believe were bouts of mania.

Mental illness was a taboo subject that was very much in the closet in those times.

School had broadened my world and given me friends. I had at least three classmates who lived on farms nearby. Learning to ride a bike had given me great adventures and an escape from the unhappiness in my home. Setting off on a winding country road, I could bike to adjacent farms. A couple of scraped knees notwithstanding, my reward was that my friends and I could explore creeks and rocks and haylofts. Not once did my friends complain about their families' monetary problems.

I was blessed to have parents who were dedicated to raising us in the Christian faith. We attended catechism during the week and mass on Sundays. Yet the predominant emotion I grew up with was guilt. I felt incredible guilt for every thought, word, or deed that seemed to cause another pain. Incredibly, it seemed that nearly all my thoughts, words, or deeds caused my parents pain. Success in school or being chosen for an honor in my community seemed to cause them pain. I soon found myself flip-flopping between worlds, trying to make authority figures happy. I became Rose the performer at school who could make good grades, laugh, sing, and play an instrument. And I learned to excel in the role most needed in my home: Rose the caretaker. The caretaker role was the only firm footing in the walking-on-eggshells atmosphere in my home. I most often took care of either my mother or my father.

Rose the caretaker did not have any needs of her own. This dedication to self-denial had actually granted me some extra attention, as my parents would point to me as an example for my siblings: "Rose never asks for anything." However, I learned that as soon as I gave up something, with uncanny regularity, something more that I dared to dream of would appear from another source. It seemed to be a matter of the heart, for when the giving was done willingly, the motive was right. It would be several years before I would come across the scripture, "For God loves a cheerful giver.[1]"

My family labeled me as lucky throughout my growing-up years and beyond, but I was certain I had hit upon a universal principle.

I was blessed with good teachers who gave me the view for the future that did not come from my home, where girls were not trained beyond cooking, sewing, and raising children. But I was to pursue my education.

The most natural selection of professions was, quite simply, that of a caretaker. What else was there? In my mind, there was not a position other than this one that was truly considered of value. Yet Rose the performer would not be content unless a challenge was presented that would allow her to do what her good teachers had taught her to do.

I decided in my teens to pursue my dream to become a registered nurse.

We had an old upright piano in the basement of our home that had once belonged to my grandmother. She had come from a talented family where every member played an instrument. However, tragedy had caused the early deaths of all three of her siblings, and since that time, my grandmother had never played the piano. My mother had inherited the instrument and was determined to produce a piano player among her children. It was decided that my brother and I would take lessons from a

---

[1] 2 Corinthians, 9:7

dedicated teacher who came to our house once a week. There was an inevitable wrestling match between my brother and me before this event, which would produce a loser who had to go first. Girls did not have a protected status in my home, and my defense was whatever I could improvise. As our teacher would often walk in on this spectacle, it is a quite a wonder that she kept coming back.

The piano was not an instrument I chose. As the music I tediously practiced drifted to the upstairs, my mother would frequently shout, "Slow down!" to my obvious attempts to get through the practice sessions as quickly as possible. My musical talent emerged later when I played the flute in high school.

I asked for, and received, a guitar for Christmas when I was twelve. After learning basic chords, I would pour out my heart in the privacy of my room, often in mournful song. I did not share my sadness with others.

I memorized the words of Henry David Thoreau when we studied *Walden* in high school: "The mass of men lead lives of quiet desperation"[2] I recognized that these people lived on my side of the street. And while where one comes from may explain a lot about you, it is not an excuse for staying there.

---

[2] Thoreau, Henry David, *Walden*, from Doren Stern, Phillip Van *The Annotated Walden*, New York, New York, Barnes and Nobles Books, 1970, p. 150

CHAPTER 4

VIEWING THE WHITE PILLARS

BEFORE I MET MY FAMILY DOCTOR, I HAD learned the definition of *awe* under the guidance of another man. At the age of seven, I had given my life to Jesus. A young priest had greatly impressed upon me that Jesus would be someone I could trust. I had seen the stained-glass windows adorning my church that depicted the stations of the cross. They depicted the agony of a sufferer. Surely this Jesus was one who could be relied upon, as I was aware of what He was willing to endure as only a seven-year-old might be. I didn't know exactly what would be involved in following Him, but the compulsion to follow was so profound that to do anything else was unthinkable.

Daniel stood out in a crowd. Most telling was the joy he radiated. It wasn't a superficial happiness but the deep, abiding fulfillment of someone who drank from streams ever flowing. His calm demeanor and careful attention to detail spoke of someone who was in service to the King. Most incredibly, he was someone who sought me out intentionally.

As I think of it now, in my child's mind, it was like being Cinderella and suddenly meeting the prince. And not unlike the tale of Cinderella, there would be the inevitable stroke of midnight, the return to rags and obscurity, and unbeknownst to me, a slipper left behind with which my prince could, incredibly, find me again.

Shortly after my decision to follow Jesus, I became ill with pneumonia that was later complicated by measles. Although I recall feeling quite sick while my fever climbed, I was actually rather excited to be in need of hospitalization. There was a great deal of monotony and tedium about the life I knew, and this offered at least a glimpse of something else. I was admitted to the pediatric floor. I had a semiprivate room with a roommate about my age.

My parents hadn't mentioned that my brothers and sisters had contracted measles and I had been exposed. There was quite an uproar when the red spots appeared on my torso and outrage from the family of the sick child in the next bed. When I was put in isolation, I had the feeling that it was punishment for something my family had collectively done. I truly wanted to make it up to these nice folks I had just met.

In my world, being good meant that I would not cry or call for help. Therefore, there was not a whimper from me when the painful penicillin shots left my legs aching. I climbed over the bedrails rather than use my call light when nature demanded that I go to the bathroom. Curiosity led me to pull the bathroom call light. When an entire floor of nurses rushed to my room, it was more attention than I dreamed of! As I recall, I repeated this activity more than once. Finally, a kindly doctor asked how he might coax me from doing this again. I asked for a rocking chair, which, incredibly, he produced. It was the end of my dangerous antics.

One of my nurses was the older sister of one of my second-grade friends, so I had a personal visit from someone who acted as a big sister to me when I most needed one. What I remember about these ladies was their smiles and the joy they radiated. In surroundings and circumstances that were far from pleasant, these overcomers had mastered the art of loving. They seemed to enjoy doing things for me, sometimes things that I could do myself. Twenty-four hours a day, never closed for weekends or holidays, they were the heart and soul of caretaking for those in desperate need.

I wondered at the core values that motivated such behavior.

The vow that I made to my Jesus was that if He would allow me to get to heaven, I would take along as many people as I could. The "if" centered around the issue of my being good, for on my side of the street, love was only forthcoming upon this condition. As I think back, this was the fundamental problem with my young theology.

Upon making this rather bold vow, I was on the path that eventually led to a registered nurse diploma. I'm certain that the influence of so many kind doctors and nurses led me to the conclusion that the best way to take along as many as I could was to enter a medical field.

After my family sold the farm and used the proceeds to fund small-town life, my getaways on my bicycle took me to a local park adjacent to a Civil War battlefield. I walked the field many times, never finding the historic relic I was seeking. What I did find as

I returned across the park was an opportunity. One of the local high-school girls was teaching baton twirling for the modest sum of fifty cents per session. My athletic tendency was intrigued with this obviously feminine pursuit that could, as it had done for the teacher, lead to an opportunity to become a majorette with the band. I could bike the distance to the park, and I had enough saved from odd jobs to buy a four-dollar baton. Later, at age thirteen, all I needed was courage to try out for the high-school twirling team. I wasn't certain I possessed the needed bravery, but perhaps my years of desperation spurred me on.

One of the requirements of the tryouts was that the twirler be able to do the scissor kick. This was a three-step windup that ended with a required kick above the head with a pointed toe. As a member of the team, I would be required to wear a heavy white leather boot while I performed this maneuver.

Little did I know as I mastered this exercise that I would later use it to defend myself while I was homeless and in and out of state hospitals.

I was absolutely thrilled to be the seventh of seven baton twirlers chosen. This endeavor would change my life, as my companions became the girls who were on the team. I formed a close friendship with one friend in particular, and her family welcomed me into their home and took me on outings. My best friend's family was from the other side of the street. There was unconditional love in her house, but there was also discipline, respect, and expectations. They loved me and encouraged me, as did many of the teachers in my school. Had it not been for those influences, I never would have found, at the age of seventeen, the courage to apply to nursing school.

As I reflect on my life, which later led to a schizoaffective/bipolar type diagnosis, I recall the many dreams I have had where there were two of me. It was perhaps at this point in my life when both identities were most evident. One of me was a performer, a baton twirler. She paid the price and practiced and earned a spot on the team, where she performed and entertained others. She never discussed her past or her family of origin. She was good at making people laugh. She could work hard and go without sleep and run eighteen miles at a time. This woman deserved to reside on the other side of the street with those who were fulfilled in life.

But the other woman was the real me. She was my private self, my identity still in progress. She did not necessarily have any intrinsic value if she could not produce. She was subject to moods and keenly aware of the reactions of others. Entirely too sensitive, she wished to be less insightful. She was capable of being negative and morose when overtired, yet she often pushed herself to the overtaxed state in an effort to show her value. She was an encourager who often encouraged the wrong person.

Not certain which side of the street she lived on, she eventually ended up in the middle of the street looking for shelter of any kind.

CHAPTER 5

AWARENESS THAT I AM NOT TO CROSS THE STREET

I AM NOT QUITE CERTAIN HOW IT WAS conveyed to me during my childhood that I had predefined limits. Perhaps it was in the very words that were spoken each day. Perhaps it was in an unspoken code of rules that demanded nothing about my home life be discussed. Certainly the rules were in place before I first attended a school.

Shame is an ugly thing. It is a veil that shrouds the identity of the one forced to wear it. A child unworthy of unconditional love is a vulnerable target in a minefield of explosive relationships. The limits imposed by this shame are actually simple yet profound in their consequences. Caught in a web of awareness that others are deserving of love while I am not, the child can only draw one of two conclusions: either those I most depend on are bad, or I am bad. The less-painful of these two choices is that I am bad.

I was well into adulthood before I began to look those I most admired directly in the eye. I stared at chins for a long time. Slowly,

I began to focus on mouths, as if I could discern true intentions by noting the way words were formed. And on upward the trek continued, until, at last, I bravely dared to meet them eye to eye.

As I reflect on the past, I recall the words *pester* and *bother*. I was not to annoy the grown-ups with my presence. Adults didn't like children, I concluded. This was probably assumed as many of my relatives had several children. But I was never certain if the sin was in creating them or inherent in the child herself. But if children were a sin and adults were not, there must be a process by which children became less sinful. I suppose this was my hope of sorts.

One day my mother was cooking when a grease fire erupted, causing second- and third-degree burns to her right hand. As she plunged her hand into cold water to counter the pain, she frantically yelled for me to go get Dr. Smith, our good neighbor across the street. Breathlessly, I ran at top speed to reach his door. Fortunately, he was home. At once, he followed me to my house, applied burn ointment, and bandaged my mother's hand, assuring her all the while that she had done the right thing from the start.

So there was, I learned, a time when it was not only permitted but necessary to cross the street because someone needed help.

Getting help for my mother became a focus and another of my life's goals. She suffered a major bout of depression and had to be hospitalized when I was seven. This was followed by a manic episode that required shock therapy. There was great shame in this occurrence judging by her words and her refusal to endure more therapy afterward. It is not unusual that this shame would be conferred upon the next generation also.

But for this new development that taught me there was a

legitimate time to cross the street, I was most grateful. It would be years before I learned to make the crossing because I needed help. It was unknown to me at the time that, in the process, I would cross the street so many times that I would comfortably and legally take up residence there.

CHAPTER 6

BIDDEN TO SIMPLY GET THE MAIL

MY DREAMS HAVE, AT TIMES, BEEN VIVID IN color and very difficult to ignore. As I reflect on this, I have to wonder whether God used such means to reach me because I was so inaccessible. I stopped trying to interpret dreams many years ago, knowing full well that the interpretation belongs to God. But I will say that often after events occur, the meaning becomes obvious to me.

The dream involving the neighbor's mansion occurred at the nadir of my life. One night, I dreamed I was playing the piano, as I had done as a child in the basement of my parents' home. I was slumped over the keyboard, mournfully producing with an apparent lack of joy. Suddenly, an angel appeared, descended the stairs, and asked me if I would cross the street and get the kind doctor's mail for him. I was more than happy to be asked to do so. I crossed the street and noticed that the mailbox was perched on a steep hill of mud, not as I remembered. I approached the hill from every angle, only to slide backward in the mud, unable to achieve my assigned task. After numerous unsuccessful strategies, I was nearly at wit's end. Determined not to leave my assignment undone, I finally took a running start and a direct approach. Not caring how much mud I was covered with, I triumphantly opened the mailbox. To my utter amazement, the envelope inside was addressed to me. Apparently the doctor's house was also my house.

Over the years, I would reflect repeatedly on this dream. The details are still vivid to me many years later. While I certainly would not advocate pondering every dream that too much television may have caused, I am also aware that God has, at times, communicated with people through dreams. Certainly, these images etched on my consciousness were a cause for reflection.

My first decision to become a nurse was just that—my decision. It was born of a dedication to works, my attempt to do something for God. As a youth, I had considered it a calling. However, my *calling* to nursing came a few years later. I think of it now as God's attempt to do something for me, the one who most needed something done.

I was working as a student nurse on a busy medical floor, and I was assigned to a patient who was perhaps in her sixties. I was told that she had bone cancer, and it was a form of cancer that was particularly painful. Of all the patients in her four-bedroom ward, she alone had no visitors. Yet she was anything but pitiful. I was surprised to see a gloriously joyful expression on her face as she sat straight upright in her bed.

As I opened her curtains to let in the morning sun, she looked outward and announced exuberantly, "The angels are coming!" The absolute certainty in her words startled me.

Only a languid blue sky and a few clouds were visible from the seventh-floor window. Yet I considered her announcement of fact as I went about my morning work. I was pleasant, although not as aware as I was about to become. I finished my morning tasks and crossed the hallway to care for another patient.

I emerged from the room to find much commotion across the hall, where I had just been. A nurse was dutifully pulling a curtain around my lady to separate her from others in the ward. I was stunned to discover that she had suddenly, unexpectedly died. But the rapturous look was still on the sweet lady's face. Much upheaval followed this event, and I was left to attend the morning routine of others. There was a sudden awareness on my part that I had been the only one privileged to know that she had literally seen the angels coming to get her.

I realized to the very core of my being that something incredible had happened. The medical had met the miraculous. Where one realm had ended, another had taken over. I realized that I was to be a witness of this. It was not a calling that I took lightly.

What does it mean to serve only because one has been asked to do so? I think, considering the dream, that it could mean significance for the one serving, not because the service was honorable but because the One being served was honorable. It is rather like being the steward of a royal household. To serve the King is no less honorable.

Reflecting now, on my dream, I have to ask myself, what about the unexpected obstacle, the mud? Had I anticipated it, I might have been less frustrated. But wasn't it a compliment to be asked to do, not that which was easy but that which was difficult?

The task was complicated by repeated setbacks until one might have simply quit and said, "It wasn't possible for me to do. I tried everything."

But what became apparent to me at that point was that I had *not* tried everything; at least one option remained.

One thing became apparent to me. There remained in my future a great victory beyond my expectations, which was abundantly beyond all that I could ask or think.

CHAPTER 7

THE NARROW GATE

Enter through the narrow gate; for the gate is wide
and the way is broad that leads to destruction, and
there are many who enter through it. (Matthew
7:13)

I WROTE A TERM PAPER WHILE ENROLLED IN
sociology my first year of college. My professor gave me an A+ and
wrote in the margin "I hope you plan to continue your education
far beyond the baccalaureate level." I was quite surprised by the
comment as I had never considered anything so lofty!

My decision to attend a three-year-diploma nursing program
after high school graduation eliminated me from most scholarship
applications, as I was not pursuing a bachelor's program. Financing
was a concern, and I had chosen something within my means.
Still, I was thrilled with my decision and determined to succeed.
I firmly believed that I was doing what the Lord had called me to
do. I was totally unaware of where this would take me.

One of my most memorable moments occurred during my psychiatric training while I attended woodshop with a group of Vietnam veterans. It was my assignment to simply attend a therapeutic activity with some of the patients. I sat quietly with a group of men in woodworking shop. I had no words to offer them, as I had no idea what they had been through, and I didn't want to pretend that I did. I sat, day by day, in silence as they worked quietly. What I learned and vowed not to forget was that war was simply too bad to talk about. After several days of soundless, solemn companionship, one of them approached me and asked if they could make something for me. I was most honored by this undeserved honor.

They used a team approach and made me a cutting board. One drew, one sawed, and one sanded. The resulting work—a delightful pig-shaped cutting board—is still a prized possession that will forever symbolize to me recovery from war.

One of my teachers, a former air force flight nurse, took me aside and told me that she felt I had a gift for psychiatric nursing. I took this compliment in stride, as I felt I was not doing more than being kind.

I married shortly after graduation, and my husband was commissioned as a second lieutenant in the army. I worked in three different states in as many nursing positions before our first child was born. I then found a part-time nursing opportunity where I could adjust my schedule around my family's needs. After the birth of our second child, my world seemed to fall apart. I began a descent into oblivion that was marked by many psychiatric admissions, and our marriage struggled. It did not survive.

I made attempts to further my education during this time, but the coveted prize of a bachelor's degree never materialized. I will say that I learned a lot. My attention turned to surviving my own personal ordeal and trying to keep my family afloat. If I survived, my children would survive. My attention was not entirely selfish, for I had seen in my family of origin that to deny the illness was to hand down the fallout to future generations. To acquire the help and the skills to survive it would be to pass on the survival strategies. I firmly believed each hospitalization would be my last.

For the first seven years of my illness, I was cared for in private clinics with private insurance dollars. The military was generous with insurance coverage. Meanwhile, my brothers and sisters in adversity were getting by with very limited resources. This became apparent to me when I lost my insurance following my divorce. A head-on collision landed me in a state hospital and with the larger, overcrowded pool of sufferers. The only course of action that I seemed to have was to eventually write about it. That task was embedded in my brain through all my trials.

At first I wrote letters. Most of them were written from one of multiple state hospitals. They were apparently crazy letters, an attempt to reach out to a world beyond myself. My choice of recipients was not wise. I have often reflected on this as a response to trauma. The mind regresses with repeated assaults, and a three-year-old was expressing herself in prose, poetry, and pictures. The recipient reminded me of family. There was never a response, although he sometimes took my phone calls. This did not deter me. I was still the little girl whose major accomplishment was simply not to need anything.

The precious jewels produced by this activity were twofold. I survived, and years later, words written then were still indelibly printed on my mind. They were words that I could now manage, and with an adult voice, I could now choose to help someone. I learned to choose the recipients of my help wisely.

When we are first aware that God has called us to a particular task, the first reaction is to emphatically deny that we could possibly have been asked to do such a thing. There were many reasons, I argued with myself, that I could not write my story and have it published.

Someone once told me that any task worthwhile that the King requests of you is always considered to be impossible. I believe this happens for two reasons. First, to achieve the objective, one has to rely on a power higher than oneself, namely the Creator who made the request. This teaches God reliance rather than self-reliance. Second, the one who receives the glory when the objective is met is the one who deserves it, namely Jesus, who died so we might be set free from the weight of guilt and shame.

CHAPTER 8

DARING TO ENTER

AS I THINK BACK ON THE EXCUSES I HAD TO not do what I clearly felt I was being asked to do, I reflect on my history of lack of control. Often, if one has lacked control over events, that individual sets out to have as much control as possible. Yet life will teach us that there are times when we can only control ourselves. I am reminded of the words of Victor Frankl, a Jewish psychiatrist who survived Auschwitz while his entire family perished at the hands of the Nazis:

> The prisoner's reaction to release can be summed up as follows: at first everything seems to him like a lovely dream; he hardly dares to believe it … How often he dreamed of his liberation— dreamed of coming home, embracing his wife, greeting his friends … to describe how he had longed for this moment of reunion, to say how many times he had dreamed of this moment, until

at last it had become a reality. And then the three blasts of the whistle shrilled in his ears ... and wrenched him out of the dream. How terrible it was to be brought back to harsh reality. But finally the day dawns when what has been longed for and dreamed of actually comes true. He cannot really enjoy his life yet—he has to learn all over again how to be happy, for he has forgotten ... in time he reaches the point where the past seems to be nothing more than a nightmare. When that time comes, he himself can no longer understand how he was able to survive the imprisonment. Henceforth he enjoys the precious feeling that after all he has experienced and suffered, there is nothing left in the world that he need fear—except perhaps, his God.[3]

Consider the positions of various people in a vehicle bound for a certain destination.

There is quite a difference between sitting in the driver's seat and being a passenger in the backseat of a vehicle. One position is a place of control; the other is a place of conveyance. We may spend years claiming our place in the front seat of a specific car of our choosing. Yet the ultimate goal is to become comfortable in the backseat of something we may or may not have chosen. We either serve our Creator in His purposes,

---

[3] Victor E. Frankl, *The Doctor and the Soul: From Psychotherapy to Logotherapy*, trans. Richard and Clary Winston, third ed. (New York: Vintage Books, 1986), 103–04.

or we spend our lives angry that we do not have the ultimate control we seek.

The driver might seem to have power over destination, direction, speed, and changes thereof. The control panel, mirrors, windows, locks, temperature, and sound system are all within the driver's command. But a passenger in the front seat might exercise some control. From this position, the passenger can clearly see the direction the driver is taking. This person might have the advantage of having the driver's ear, so to speak. The influence exercised might also determine where the car is headed or determine a route taken or adjust the speed. In fact, in actuality, depending on how much the driver values the passenger's input, the passenger might be the navigator who exerts more control than the driver. Thus, appearances can be deceptive.

The backseat passenger is a traveler who may or may not have an end in mind. Hopefully this person likes the intended destination, as a choice to exit the car would certainly result in bodily harm unless the driver agrees to stop. Yet the backseat passenger would seem to have very little control. In fact, this passenger might be totally surprised at where the journey ends.

I bring these considerations to mind because of the many dreams I have had involving an automobile, not an uncommon dream theme.

Between periods of illness, I reentered the workforce. I dreamed that I was driving a car and my two children were in the backseat dressed for the journey with matching pink and blue gym bags. I was traveling along the coast on the sand where there was no defined road while the waves crashed upon the beach in a regular cycle. I was fearful yet hopeful and determined.

I would get warnings of impending mania through dreams. On a few occasions, my car would be in reverse, out of control, without brakes. Only an inevitable crash would slow the vehicle. Such a dream would usually end in a hospitalization. A few years later, I would dream of driving my car and would notice a light flashing on my dashboard. It was the inevitable signal to pull over and get help. At this point in my life, I could predict with accuracy when I needed to slow down to prevent the inevitable crash of the illness cycle.

But there were also times when I was either the front-seat or the backseat passenger. Forced to give up the control I craved, I could only trust the One who has ultimate control.

As my circle of influence widened, my dreams would find me on a bus. I was not the driver. There were perhaps thirty others, all traveling to the same destination. At this point in my life, I was an involved member of my church and community.

What does it mean to serve? It often seemed to me that the process of overcoming my past had consumed all of my energy, time, and resources. It was difficult to relate to a classmate who had graduated magna cum laude with an advanced degree who was successfully climbing a ladder. Beyond my associate's degree, the only degrees I have known are the various degrees of mental anguish I have had to rise above.

I always thought I needed at least a master's degree to write the book I felt I was being asked to write. This thought occurred repeatedly in the days before I learned to be myself and before I learned to flow with God's plan and not my own. Being asked to sit in the backseat is often a position of meekness, and before honor comes humility.[4]

It is precisely this lack of control that I have had to come to terms with. I have to trust the driver. This trust has not come easily for me. Trust is what was essentially missing from my early relationships. Learning who to trust was a skill I previously lacked. It was not a task easily accomplished but a skill painstakingly acquired. Yet there was no other way. My fears of being rejected or abandoned would often rise up from the swamp of my past emotions. Would things be different now? Was I on the right bus headed for the right place? Was I sitting where I was being asked to sit?

Were my emotions of fear a response to, once again, choosing the wrong vehicle? Or was I simply responding to being outside my previous zone of comfort?

When I was in my twenties, being outside my zone of comfort showed itself in relating to authority figures. I recall breaking out in a cold sweat whenever, as a nurse, I was approached by a doctor. As I look back, it is nothing short of incredible to me that I kept trying. That same feeling would accompany me with every new field I entered. Employed at a much-needed job in an office of real-estate appraisers, I was terrified of my lack of office and people skills and my fear of failure. That I learned enough to make a good housing investment was in itself astonishing. Slowly, over time, I have learned to predict and expect my reaction to new situations. Many of my fears, though unfounded, are based on past events. And although I no longer live in the past, I would be lying to you if I said I was not influenced by it. This bothered me unnecessarily,

---

[4] Proverbs 15:33

this inability to move entirely past the past. But I learned that God's grace is given in spite of, not because of. Paul had his thorn in the flesh,[5] and certainly, I have mine. No matter how fervently I *have* prayed that it might be removed, it has remained so I might learn His grace is sufficient.[6]

I said yes to being willing to serve. I found the courage to do what I felt I was being asked to do without any excuses.

---

[5] 2 Corinthians 12:7
[6] 2 Corinthians 12:9

CHAPTER 9

DECIDING TO STROLL
BY THE GARDEN

WHILE I WAS HOSPITALIZED FOR PERHAPS the fifteenth time—before I made drastic changes—I came upon a poem by Portia Nelson from "There's a Hole in My Sidewalk."[7] It spoke loudly to me.

Autobiography in Five Chapters

Chapter One
I walk down the street.
There is a deep hole in the sidewalk.
I fall in.
I am lost ... I am hopeless.
It isn't my fault.

---

[7] Portia Nelson, *There is a Hole in My Sidewalk,* "Autobiography in Five Chapters," http//www.inspiration line.com/rss/10OCT 2005 htm, (accessed April 2, 2011).

It takes forever to find a way out.

Chapters 2, 3, and 4 are a progression of chapter one. The one walking down the sidewalk continues to walk down the same street. I saw myself falling in again and again, although I finally reached the conclusion that this has become a habit. So, it is now my fault. Finally, we come to the last chapter.

Chapter Five

I walk down a *different* street.

When my thoughts were dark, there was no future. It was as if a wall had gone up and my only view was a sea of gray thoughts into eternity. I was a prisoner of this mindset. I would have been angry at someone had I the right to be angry. As it was, I had no rights. I deserved every rude comment that came my way. After all, I was a despicable specimen of humanity. For one who held so much promise at an earlier age, one who wanted to save the world, I had reduced myself to a miserable existence that inconvenienced everyone around me. Mostly, I was selfish and lazy, the labels pinned on me in my early childhood. Who could save me from such a curse? Could my Jesus save me, or had I committed the unpardonable sin? I wasn't certain which one that was, but I was certain I must have committed it. Was my decision to follow Christ as a child a lie? Or was I simply riding in the backseat of a vehicle driven by an uncertain driver? If so, the destination was most surely hell.

Then, after months of gray skies and a determination beyond my own strength, a glimmer of light would shine through until it was a powerful, illuminating light. My relief at those moments was indescribable, and my behaviors were erratic and sometimes impulsive, seemingly without logic. While the professionals would accuse me of not taking my medication (but I thought I had), I would wait for the vision that would appear on the mountaintop. I often spent the mountaintop in the psychiatric ward of a hospital, but nevertheless, it was a mountaintop. There was a purpose to my existence, and it was unique. I was loved beyond my ability to comprehend. I was suffering as my Savior had suffered. Who would not have been honored to stand on the mountaintop with my Lord? On one of these impatient bouts of mania, after antipsychotic medication brought me to an even keel from impulse-driven danger, the vision became to write everything that came to me. I recorded my thoughts, dreams, and hopes, expressing myself in poetry and prose. This new assignment kept me occupied in what some might have considered to be God-forsaken places.

Yet with dreams on paper in front of me, I couldn't for the life of me understand the pull that was holding me back.

A friend once took me digging for clams, and he used the parable of crabs in a bucket to describe my situation to me. I had never heard the parable, and it provided much to ponder.

"When several crabs are in a bucket," he told me, "they all want out. But every time one climbs to the top of the bucket to escape, the other crabs collectively pull it downward. After several attempts, the climber frequently decides that it is futile to climb."

Thus, the only vision becomes the wall, the confinement of the bucket. The wall literally allows no view of something better.

It was at this point in my life that I began to withdraw from situations I previously considered it wrong for a nurse to withdraw from. I began to keep my work at work and limit my role as a rescuer to situations that were professional. I acknowledged that the private Rose needed time to pause and reflect. I found safe relationships. I left the risky interactions, no matter how much I felt inclined to help. I prayed that I no longer let others pull me back downward into the bucket.

As God is no respecter of persons,[8] the same freedom is available to anyone who feels confined to walls of imprisonment. A life that is well lived is one of overcoming. Adversity is not a sign that it was never meant to be but a signpost that you are indeed on the correct path.

Try. Try something else. Try something new. Try a new angle. Try what you have not tried. Try using mentors who have succeeded. Try with the light of scripture that has not been tainted with human error—words you have researched and not passively accepted.

A vision is much more than that which you assume to be humanly possible. In fact, if it is humanly possible, it is not a vision at all. It must be seen and believed and rehearsed with words of faith and hope. It must be nurtured with love. Human love with its limitations cannot supply what only the almighty Creator can supply.

Walk down a different sidewalk and avoid falling into a hole. Become whole.

Then, with renewed strength and determination, climb out of the bucket.

---

[8] Acts 10:34

CHAPTER 10

SERVANT OF THE LORD'S MANSION

I WAS ON DISABILITY AND OUT OF THE WORK force for over five years. The first step on the climb out of poverty seemed unattainable. I began with a change of attitude.

There was an inspiring view of a magnificent mountain from my rather rundown section-eight apartment complex. I was receiving food stamps, and a new supermarket had recently been built within walking distance. I had a Pell grant to finish my associate's degree and a free bus pass. I lived in the United States of America. I was, according to the world's standards, rich indeed. I thanked God for my immense wealth, which included living where opportunity and freedom abound. During one manic episode that ended in hospitalization, I played Lee Greenwood's "God Bless the U.S.A." at a loud volume to my listening neighbors, many of whom were caught up in drugs, theft, and the other vices of those who remain downtrodden.

I was well aware that I needed to take advantage of every opportunity, even when I was uncomfortable with the task. I cared for neighbors who were in need. I worked as a volunteer in the safety office of a hospital, although it was not in my area of expertise. I took a course in building a résumé, completely baffled as to how my résumé could appear to be anything desirable after so long an absence from work.

I put in applications again and again that were turned down. Finally, at the end of my pride, I prayed and fasted for a job.

I was offered a part-time position that paid eight dollars per hour. It was in a field totally foreign to me, although I can now look back and see God's handiwork. I worked as an assistant to a real estate appraiser. Within a few months the position became full time, and I was able to move to an apartment closer to my work. From that position, I had plans to return to work as a registered nurse, as impossible as it seemed. Within a year I was hired by a very needy nursing home that had been desperate for staff.

I bought a used car. I soaked every decision with guidance and prayer.

Eventually, I was able to buy a very old, very small house in a prime location in a valley, as recommended by the appraiser I worked for. I had to work two jobs to finance it. Within three years I was able to work enough overtime in nursing to drop the second job. Unknown to me at the time, the equity in this investment would provide needed funds for my two teenagers, who lived with their father. It would also provide the resources I needed to relocate.

The Lord was with me; He had not forgotten me. I had been forgiven for the years I had wasted and the time I lost. My simplistic faith was growing to become the needed tool for the time I had left.

This remaining time would be filled with success God's way.

CHAPTER 11

THE SERVANT'S CLOTHING

Memories of an earlier time, a much more prosperous time, came back to me. I was contemplating the seeming success of those years after so many years of surviving.

I graduated from nursing school at the ripe age of twenty. I remembered that in my first registered nurse job, I usually drank old coffee, which often became cold coffee. The habit started when I first worked the night shift in my hometown hospital. It was a small hospital with only two floors. I worked the second floor, which included labor and delivery, the nursery, and female surgical patients. A fresh pot of coffee at eleven at night became the caffeine I needed at three in the morning. Often without needed time to brew more, I drank the high-octane variety that was readily available.

In my leisure time, I always dressed in blue jeans, T-shirts, and very unfussy attire. My husband and I lived in an apartment next to the hospital, and I vividly recall being called in for an emergency on my day off. We did not own a washer and dryer, and all of my uniforms were in the dirty laundry, yet to be washed. So I pulled on my non-work and covered it all with what I considered to be a respectable white lab coat. I was asked to help in the ER, where a young epileptic and quite inebriated patient was lying on an exam table, yelling at anyone who approached him. As I was puncturing his skin for the needed intravenous line, despite my explanations as to why he needed my help, the patient suddenly punched me in the arm.

He began to shout, "I don't want some young candy striper working on me!"

I'm not sure how the change occurred, but that it did is nothing short of miraculous to me. Over the years, a transformation occurred, first in my mind and later in my demeanor.

In my late thirties, having begun the work of recovery from my illness, I was sitting in the office of a business owner who genuinely cared for his employees. I first noticed his generosity. Every morning he walked next door to a coffee shop and purchased the latte of one's choosing, and a large one at that. My preference was for a mocha, and I always requested a small. He consistently brought me a large. I remember the delicious aroma of the steaming cup of kindness, and I first considered the word *abundance*. The delicacy that I could not afford appeared every morning, and I would savor every drop of this fatness in my lean state. One day, the morning chatter in the office turned to credit cards. I had announced that after bankruptcy had reduced me to cash only, my credit had finally been restored to the point that I had been offered a credit card. I had no intention of using it except for emergencies concerning my family.

The subject then turned to clothing, in particular, *my*

clothing. I had rationalized that rumbling through thrift shops was a way of life that I preferred. Certainly, I was grateful that it was an option for me. I was surprised when my coworkers suggested that I could use a credit card to buy new clothes. It was suggested in such a way that I did not feel I was being *required to* have the new attire to improve business. It would rather be a reward I would give myself for the hard work of getting back into the workforce.

I mused over the idea.

I put a great deal of thought into my decision to show up at a clothing store I had previously considered not to be in my league on a sale day. I also computed how much I could spend and yet pay off the balance without incurring any interest. I had decided just what I needed. The advantage of sifting through so many thrift shops and then meeting so many business associates made my decision simple.

I decided that, as I did not yet have a need for nursing uniforms, I would buy something dignified, maybe even a business suit. It was long way from where I had started, but it seemed most likely a preparation for where I was intended to go. I found clothes that were feminine yet professional, and I admit to feeling that there was more to life than I had previously known as I tried them on. I laughed to myself that God does indeed have a sense of humor. Who would have thought that the girl from the farm who grew up with the chickens would ever be clothed in anything so nice? The word *abundance* again entered my mind. *What is the scripture,* I asked myself, *that would support a change of plans beyond stale coffee and blue jeans?* Once again, I rehearsed the scripture I had committed to memory:

Now to Him who is able to do far more abundantly
beyond all that we ask or think, according to the
power that works within us, to Him *be* the glory
in the church and in Christ Jesus to all generations
forever and ever. (Ephesians 3:20)

This was not about me. It was all about His plans to bring
glory to His name.

Later, I bought the perfect accessory for my purchases. It was
something every professional in the office owned: a black leather
briefcase. I admit that this extravagance took some faith and
courage to purchase. And yet I felt I was being asked to do so. It
became a symbol of what I was being asked to do, as impossible as
it seemed at the time. It would be at least six years before I would
use it, first to hold résumés and travel plans as I moved across the
country. Later, it was necessary to hold new copies of my books in
case the store ran out at my book signings.

I recalled another dream I had while I was an inpatient in a
state hospital during a time of tremendous loss. I was at a garage
sale, and a banner above my head read: "Would you give up
everything you have for everything you ever wanted?" People
were walking away with all of my things, and I didn't feel that I
had the right to stop them. Finally, I saw a young girl carry off
my medical-surgical textbook. I had purchased it myself at the
age of eighteen and studied it exhaustively. I stood up to retrieve
it! Suddenly two angels appeared, one on each side of me. They
simply asked me to sit down.

I obediently complied. When I did so, I saw the items I once
held in my hope chest. Too close to the ground to be noticed, I

saw two pillowcases, two much-used dish towels, and a large quilt. But I also saw a black leather case. The case held a flute that I once played. I put the three pieces of the instrument together.

And I played a little Thanksgiving tune.

CHAPTER 12

TRYING TO REACH THE MAILBOX

WHILE I WAS BLESSED WITH INSURANCE TO cover therapy in the early years of my illness, I was reduced to what government healthcare for the poor could provide later on. I think in my case, both approaches were needed. The first provision taught me to seriously look at myself. The later dilemma I found myself in taught me to look everywhere but myself.

I began to work with an open admission of bipolar illness. Eventually I would work in nursing homes for ten years. The workload was often heavy, and the limitations on my schedule mandated by my doctor seemed to keep me mostly healthy, if not always popular with the administration.

My salary was always short of what was needed. I was at the very bottom of the pay scale. Yet my dedication to tithing and beyond had led me to trust in God's provision. Always needing to make a house payment kept me financially solvent and completely dedicated to keeping myself healthy, despite anyone's objections to the contrary.

When I was not yet at the point I would have called myself recovered, I had bouts of illness that caused me to be hospitalized or otherwise unable to work. In due course, I worked with a young man suffering from posttraumatic stress disorder.

He was not yet a US citizen, and this former soldier from Liberia was only nineteen. Working as a nursing assistant, I first noticed his command of the English language. I next noticed his constant movement and distractibility. He was—quite obviously to me—reliving something that left him completely unable to focus on anything else. In time, over a coffee break, he confided that he had been forced to serve in the Liberian Army from the ages of fourteen to eighteen. He described how men came through his village recruiting young boys to serve. Laughing at himself, he described how he and his friends were most honored to be given a weapon and a uniform. Solemnly and sadly, he confessed that of all his friends, he had been the only one to survive. In the end, his unit was totally overrun, and he had escaped by literally running for his life.

He acknowledged that Jesus Christ was his Savior. His mother had come to the United States a few years prior and was working as a licensed practical nurse. She had met him at the embassy and managed to get him out of the country. She brought him to the United States.

My research in trauma, in an effort to be of some help, became the missing piece of my own unsolved puzzle.

I attempted to convince my young friend that his symptoms might be helped with medication, which would improve his concentration, or a support group that allowed him to speak of the horrors he had seen. He did not have the resources to seek either.

One night, the directors of the facility produced the jacket required by his job title that my young friend had consistently refused to wear. The management could only be tolerant for so long. He was told, point-blank, that he would either wear the jacket or be relieved of his job. Knowing the details of his past and the particular hideousness of being forced to wear a uniform, what little I could say fell on deaf ears. He wore the jacket most reluctantly, his behavior becoming louder and wilder throughout the evening. Near the end of his shift, he wildly and dramatically ripped the jacket to shreds in full view of the entire staff. He was promptly fired.

How should someone in need of professional help seek help? My only suggestion is prayerfully. Good therapy is not so much lying on a couch and telling what one does not want to tell (while this might be part of it) as it is sitting upright and hearing what one does not want to hear.

I recall a young woman high in the throes of mania who appeared at my church one evening. She waltzed through every small group meeting excitedly talkative and very loud. In each group, she announced her own knowledge of scripture and opinions, which had, in part, led her down the path she was on. She was living in a hotel, squandering the inheritance she had recently received, and would be penniless shortly.

One of the church elders came to me after her first few visits and said quite earnestly, "We don't know what to do with her."

Not wanting her to leave the safe domain of the church and yet not knowing exactly how to handle the situation, they approached me as a last resort. I admit that I felt totally at a loss as to how to help her.

She was involved in outpatient counseling and was seeing a caseworker, but from my own experience, I imagined her caseworker would be overstretched. Not acting in a professional capacity but as a friend, I simply decided to try to get to know her. I gave her rides to church and eventually asked if she would like to join me for a meal. She agreed and chose a diner that was smoky, crowded, and apparently comfortable for her. It became our get-together location for a few months. At the end of that time, she showed signs of trusting me, although minimally. We traded information on our family situations, and she consistently referred to her situation as "fine." She insisted that just as she was "fine," everything in her childhood had also been "fine." Eventually I learned just how fine that had been.

Her father had kidnapped her from her grandparents' home. He had lost custody after her mother had committed suicide while she was a toddler. He often locked her in a closet and fed her with food shoved under the door. She was quite certain that he was a nice guy. He often took her out of the locked space so they could bathe together. Apparently the grandparents had not battled to get her back. But after his death when she was a teenager, she returned to her grandparents. The inheritance she had all but spent was from them.

Her only living relative was a distant aunt. I was introduced to this isolated woman, who spent all of her time and money on her two small dogs. Her relationship with her niece was one of resigned tolerance; they did not seem to share an emotional attachment. It was obvious to me that her niece's illness was definitely not a burden the aunt wished to bear, which seemed to make the niece scream all the louder for the attention she needed.

This young woman seemed to lack any insight into her problems. I was at a loss as to what I was being asked to do. She showed me her room and a very dedicated study of scripture that she had undertaken. I encouraged her along those lines.

One night, she called me in desperation and shouted over the phone that she was planning to kill herself. She had made previous attempts at suicide, so from her tone of voice and her history, I took her very seriously. I talked with her, and the tone of my voice was stern and somber. I prayed with her over the phone for a resolution to her crisis. I told her to call her caseworker after we hung up. I continued to pray for her after our conversation ended.

The next time we spoke, she was in jail. She had stabbed one of her aunt's dogs. I spoke to her about the seriousness of what she had done. Sensing that my small part was over, I left her to those who were in charge of her case. I continue to pray for her.

I became aware that at least her attendance at our church was a plea for help.

When I first became severely depressed, I first sought the help of a psychiatric clinic. I have often reflected on this decision and wondered if my course would have been shorter had I first gone to my church. At the time, I was a practicing Catholic, and I did seek help through confession and prayer. But there was no one who could specifically help with counseling. I decided that psychiatric care and faith were not incompatible; one could bolster the other. Not everyone agrees with me.

Years later, in another denomination in another church, I was part of a Wounded Heart class, which is specifically for those who have experienced sexual abuse of some kind. A woman joined our group who was barely in the room, so completely unable was she to share. It became obvious to me that her depression was so severe that our group alone was not going to be enough to reach her. Worse yet was the reaction of some of the members to her condition. One member blatantly told her that her mood was incompatible with her faith, implying that she should snap out of it. Apparently, this member had only read selected passages of the Bible, as I am aware that Job, David, and the writer of Ecclesiastes experienced what could only be described as severe depression. In this woman's case, I felt she needed more than our group, and I met with her privately and told her so. I decided that my own original course of professional help was necessary for me.

One thing is certain: if a wall of mud stands between you and the master plan for your life, you need help to get past it. You need the assistance of at least one other and sometimes, several others.

CHAPTER 13

A MUDDY HILL

AFTER SURVIVING AN ORDEAL WHILE ON THE streets, I first sought the free services of a mental health professional who was available through my place of employment. Before I divulged the whole of what I had experienced, I offered a small token, a bit like putting one's toe in the water before taking the plunge. He told me with a wink of the eye that I needed to return for another visit. He confessed that I didn't necessarily need help, but "I just like you and want to see you again."

I never went back.

In the process of recovery, I saw psychiatrists, psychologists, social workers, nurses, caseworkers, pastors, lay workers, policemen, and friends. Not all were empathetic. Not all were helpful.

From age twenty-six to thirty-eight, I had approached my diagnosis from every angle, much like my attempts to climb the muddy hill in my dream. The task I most wanted to complete, that which I was being asked to do, was dependent upon my reaching the mailbox.

First, I tried total compliance, locked into the psychiatric community like a ping-pong ball still on the table. Bouncing from one paddle to another, I had no input or emotion, as if this would somehow be safe. When this failed, I tried denial, as if, failing in my first attempt, I would simply refuse to have a diagnosis. As the resulting losses mounted, I finally found my rage, understandable yet uncontrolled, as if raging at the world would be enough to change it. And when my rage would end in another disaster, once again, I would become hopelessly compliant.

I had come full circle, and nothing had worked.

In the end, I had lots of records. I had inpatient records, commitment records, outpatient records, court records, professional license records, and police records.

My life was a huge crime scene with red tape reading, "Keep out." My admittance to the respectable world seemed to be far beyond this barrier. I was clueless as to how to move past the tape.

It seemed an impossibility.

Committed, caring Christians, some of them in the psychiatric community, had dared to suggest that I needed to deal with my anger. Recognizing this truth but feeling powerless to move past it, I asked how that might be done. They suggested to me that praying for those who had hurt me was the solution. I thought I had prayed for them previously. But I became aware that my prayers had stopped when the hurt had become intense. I was forced to find the forgiveness that reaches beyond the easy graces and extends to the utmost. It is not reached quickly or cheaply but painfully. As

I identify the sinner in me capable of inflicting the same wounds, I find the love for my enemy that is needed.

In this process of forgiving, incredibly, I found something else. It was the baby not to be thrown out with the dirty bathwater. Needing to accept help from so many, and aware of the different attitudes toward me, I had slowly and steadily developed the discernment that was previously absent when choosing relationships. This most-needed gift had been developing all along, unknown to me. With every encounter of assistance from another, I had come away with a precious jewel of wisdom.

Finally, with the support of safe relationships, I tried the direct approach. I took a running start and approached the muddy hill, as if my purpose in life was to do just that. I admitted that I had bipolar disorder and that it had the potential to destroy my life. But I also acknowledged my strengths and my willingness to learn from the past and use it to shape my future.

I was on the bottom rung of the career ladder for nurses. I had been grateful for the bottom rung. But I was suddenly inspired to try for more so I would be better able to help my family financially. All my children and their spouses, as well as my grandchildren, were being faced with expenses related to fighting a war of their own.

After September 11, 2001, my son and son-in law were involved in the War on Terror. I wanted to do my part.

I took a position working as a nurse in the Veteran's Administration nursing home. All was well for about a month until I was called into a manager's office. Why had I not disclosed a misdemeanor in my past? The simple answer was that I did not know I had one. I had been accused of breaking a no-contact order and had pled guilty. When it became apparent that I had a record, I contacted my lawyer and was able to get the charge expunged.

I was asked to return to my position at the nursing home when the record was cleared, but I decided not to. I considered at that point that it might be possible to clear my name in other areas with records. "Well done, my faithful servant," was at the top of a muddy hill, and I refused to slide backward in any more muck.

Prayerfully, I admitted my powerlessness to succeed in my own strength. This approach did not come easily, as the church of my youth was a church of works. I had been taught that succeeding always involved more and more work on the part of the one trying. I was now learning the process of waiting on the Lord. It seemed to me that putting one foot in front of the other, having only enough light for each day, was more closely related to trust than attempting something drastic in nature. I combined this waiting with the knowledge that I was completely forgiven as a redeemed child of my Father. Jesus had paid the supreme price by dying for my sins. I encouraged myself with scripture. I found a good church with members who would encourage me. I read books by those who had solved the problem of bipolar illness. I read about recovery from trauma. I paid attention to dreams that were profound and detailed, such that they were meant to be remembered. I acknowledged that interpretation belongs to God. I found a doctor I liked and would listen to, and I took my medicine as prescribed. I let my close friends know that there was a problem I was in the process of solving. I leaned on them.

If through discernment I concluded that another would not be understanding, I said nothing. The exception to this was my employer. I felt I owed them the truth. There were positions that

I left, but in the end, God always opened another more fulfilling, more prosperous door. I learned, in the process of revealing, that others who were limited by shame would often confide in me. My attempts to reach out to them eventually led to success.

In the first of several struggles to clear my name of records, I found the end of waiting. It was now time:

> Though youths grow weary and tired,
> And vigorous young men stumble badly,
> Yet those who wait for the Lord
> Will gain new strength;
> They will mount up *with wings* like eagles,
> They will run and not get tired,
> They will walk and not become weary.[9]

---

[9] Isaiah 40:30–31

CHAPTER 14

WILL I ALWAYS BE COVERED WITH THIS MUD?

How does one arrive at the point where opinions of the wrong critics matter but little? I had always been a rather sensitive child, one who tried entirely too hard to please those around me. The journey from childhood to adulthood took me longer than I care to admit. In the process, I learned to value the opinions of a select few and tune out the rest. To pretend we will live this life without enemies is naïve indeed.

And yet, there is this scriptural promise: "When a man's ways are pleasing to the Lord, He makes even his enemies to be at peace with him."[10]

In the process of trudging through walls of mud, we learn something profound. We recognize ourselves as sinners. This revelation was most apparent to me because of the many other sufferers I had been unable or unwilling to help. Slick with the

---

[10] Proverbs 16:7

grime of refuse, I had certainly noticed others covered in the same filth, but I was often powerless to be of assistance

We have on occasion been mudslingers ourselves. Through God's mercy, we arrive at a place where we are showered with the pure springs of grace. It should be apparent that this great benevolence was through no effort of our own. Only the merciful compassion of the One who literally died in our place has earned us this fresh, clean slate. This same rebirth of purity is available to every sinner, and our noble task is to simply share the good news.

The great dichotomy of our slate wiped clean is that we are still sinners in need of grace. We struggle as we walk through a sinful world, getting our feet filthy. The words of Jesus as He washed the feet of His disciples were, "You are clean, but not all of you."[11] He was speaking of Judas, one of His disciples with whom He had spent three years in close companionship. Judas had seen firsthand the love Jesus radiated, the miracles He performed, the absolute authority with which He spoke. In the end, Judas betrayed Him, yet none of the disciples knew of whom Jesus spoke.

In their own ways, they would all betray Him. However, all but Judas would accept the forgiveness Jesus was so ready to extend. All but Judas would humble themselves to realize that Jesus, the sinless One, would die as the substitute for the death they deserved.

It is precisely this identification with a sinful world that is meant to give us our needed humility.

Certainly, there are critical opinions that matter. But even so, I should not be living my life so as to gain your good opinion of me. My life is to be lived by attending to the task at hand with just

---

[11] John 13:10b

enough light for each day to take the needed step that leads me in the direction of the next day. This does not mean I am clueless as to where I am going. It does mean that I know what my Lord promises. I trust Him, day by day, to get me there.

> No longer do I call you slaves, for the slave does not know what his master is doing; but I have called you friends, for all things that I have heard from My Father I have made known to you.[12]

At some point in my adult life, I began to see the Lord's justice. He answered concerns I could only leave to Him. He does eventually repay. And indeed, He will not be mocked. I truly began to pity the lost who were suffering the effects of just retribution. At about the same time, I came to understand my role as an intercessor. Many of those who were brought across my path were those I was meant to quite simply and earnestly pray for. Our experience of unanswered prayer is often unrecognized, for God does indeed answer. Sometimes the answer is no; He might say yes to something else. Thus, we don't have the proper respect for the power of prayer precisely because of our sinfulness.

Prayer is not a litany of wants repeated by a beggar. Prayer is meant to be a two-way conversation between a frail child and a God the child adores, is eternally grateful to, and is most eager to listen to. This does not mean that what we hear will always be easy to hear, for the sinner in a fallen world can fall prey to fallen desires that keep one far from the mark. Course correction can be difficult indeed.

---

[12] John 15:15

Will I always be covered with this mud? The answer, quite simply, is yes and no.

Every saint has a past, but every sinner who has dedicated his or her life to Jesus has a future. While Satan, known as the accuser, will constantly remind you of your history, the word of God is meant to constantly spark hope for your future. We are not meant to dwell on what we did or what we might have done. If there are apologies to be made or restitution to be paid, then forgive and pay up and get on with your life. The words of Paul sum it up:

> Not that I have already obtained *it* or have already become perfect, but I press on so that I may lay hold of that for which also I was laid hold of by Christ Jesus. Brethren, I do not regard myself as having laid hold of *it* yet; but one thing I *do;* forgetting what *lies* behind and reaching forward to what *lies* ahead, I press on toward the goal for the prize of the upward call of God in Jesus Christ.[13]

I would like to tell you that I learned all of this rather quickly and immediately set about getting on with my life. Alas, this was not my case. I slid backward down the muddy hill many times before I finally took that deep breath and running start to assault the mud directly. Only then did I meet with the success I knew was to be mine.

All of this brings us to the question of how to live peaceably with mudslinging enemies. It is not as if we serve a God who

---

[13] Philippians 3:12–13

doesn't see. It is precisely our response that our enemies are weighing. Just how riled are we, those of us who sport the white badge of Christian? The business of turning the other cheek can be difficult indeed. This matter of living peaceably has to do with trusting our God who sees:

> BE ANGRY, AND *yet* DO NOT SIN; do not let the sun go down on your anger, and do not give the devil an opportunity. [14]

> Therefore, since we have so great a cloud of witnesses surrounding us, let us also lay aside every encumbrance and the sin which so easily entangles us, and let us run with endurance the race that is set before us, fixing our eyes on Jesus, the author and perfecter of faith, who for the joy set before Him endured the cross, despising the shame, and has sat down at the right hand of the throne of God.[15]

> It is not a job for the faint of heart.

---

[14] Ephesians 4:26
[15] Hebrews 12:1–2

CHAPTER 15

THE DIRECT APPROACH

FORGIVING OTHERS IS OFTEN MUCH EASIER than forgiving oneself. I recall waking early one morning on my climb out of misery with these words ringing in my ears: When I forgive, I forgive completely.

Just as I do not contemplate every dream I recall upon awakening, I do not put stock in all words resounding in my head. But I am also aware that the Holy Spirit can speak in many ways. This was definitely a time I chose to reflect.

I began earnest soul-searching for anyone I had not yet forgiven. Only one person came to mind: me.

I had, perhaps, partially forgiven myself. This came with an "as long as" clause. But life lived is full of failure, and it is inevitable both before you as well as behind you. The best anyone can do is learn from the mistakes and move on without more repetition. And even with this determination, there may be a recurrence. This inevitably comes with guilt and more shame at having failed again.

There is only One who can set you free from true guilt. He died a sinless death on a cross with arms outstretched wide, as if to say, "I love you this much." It only occurs when we first admit that we are powerless in our own strength to overcome our failings. We must ask for *His* strength and *His* grace. It is the only way we succeed.

Peter vividly demonstrated this inability to move past his deficiencies despite his declarations of love and loyalty to Jesus. Though he was once confident of his own power, he was humbled to the point that he returned to fishing. Jesus sought to reinstate the leader who had denied Him thrice with three simple questions:

> "Simon, *son* of John, do you love Me more than these?" He said to Him, "Yes, Lord; You know that I love You. He said to Him, "Tend my lambs."

> He said to him again a second time, "Simon *son* of John, do you love Me?" He said to Him, "Yes Lord; You know that I love You." He said to him, "Shepherd my sheep." He said to him the third time, "Simon *son* of John, do you love Me?" Peter was grieved because He said to him the third time, "Do you love me?" And he said to Him, "Lord, You know all things; You know that I love You." Jesus said to him, "Tend my sheep."[16]

And Peter, the rock, did just that.

Where had I started from? Had I not loved Jesus since I was

---

[16] John 21:15b–17

a child? And yet the choices I made were not wise—the choices of a lost child. The blessings I was given despite my choices were also obvious to me. I had been given good teachers, education, good health care, and precious children followed by precious grandchildren.

I began to research bipolar illness from all sources available. Some were practical, some were spiritual, some were medical, and some were only theoretical. I valued input from trusted others.

A couple of incidents finally freed the woman who had once been so out of control. My work with patients in nursing homes and, later in rehabilitation from brain injuries, had allowed me to experience others who were frequently out of control. Often, the condition can be corrected with medication and environmental changes. But what was interesting to me was the reaction of those closest to the patient. They seemed to fit into one of two categories. Either the family had the resources and emotional strength to deal with the behaviors, or they simply did not. If that strength was in place, the recovery would inevitably be hastened. If it was not present, the recovery was usually more complicated. The patient often became dependent on an overcrowded, impersonal system of aftercare where outcomes were less certain.

Rose the nurse finally viewed Rose the former patient with compassion.

The second thing that happened against the odds was the tremendous healing and growth I saw in my children. I had survived, and they, in turn, had survived.

The word *direct* was one I often contemplated. It means "unswerving" or "undeviating." There was no pretense at being anything other than I was. I was the me that my God had in mind when He created me. The price for this woman had already been paid. Who was I to complain that she had cost too much?

I love Mary Magdalene. This woman is one few would have wanted to keep company with, either before or after Jesus healed her tormented mind. This is evident after her conversion precisely because she wasn't believed when she reported the tomb was empty.[17] I imagine that the other disciples were tolerant at best of this woman's presence. But believing her report was another matter. And yet she was given the distinct honor of first seeing the resurrected Christ, and there would be no doubt afterward of God's opinion of her. Jesus had mercy on this woman and had expelled seven demons from her.[18] The question in the mind of the healthy might be, "What does one *do* that seven demons might take up residence in a soul?" A better question, perhaps the very one that Jesus asked, might be, "What is *experienced* by the one in anguish that seven demons would have such a stronghold?"

---

[17] Mark 16:11
[18] Luke 8:2

CHAPTER 16

FINDING MY NAME ON THE ENVELOPE

THERE WAS A TIME IN MY LIFE WHEN I DIDN'T know just what God had in mind regarding all the adversity in my life. My hopes were mediocre at best, sprinkled with moments of manic inspiration and grandeur. But by the grace of God, I was to find the inspiration-led goals and leave the mania behind. I was understandably excited about the new horizon that loomed before me.

I wanted most to be a good wife and mother. Then I wanted to serve my community in a duty-bound, consistent manner in a loving home that would provide comfort and encouragement to all who entered. I wanted to be a good nurse, whatever that duty might entail. These were simple goals, yet lofty.

I had considered that I had failed at not one, but all of these aspirations. And yet it was my precious Lord who knew and approved of my ambitions and was intent on giving me the desires of my heart no matter the impossibilities that seemed most evident. I was quite simply to be His willing vessel.

It was my willingness to serve that eventually led to success. There was a time when this willingness quite simply meant compliance to treatment in submission to those in authority over me. I remember God dealing with me on this issue. At the time, I was without a job, a home, or my children. My argument with the Creator, a futile exercise in vanity, was, "Look where submission to treatment has taken me." Our obedience is still required although we may not understand it. I was silver in the fire of refinement. Years later, an event occurred that explained, in part, what God had been doing while I was complaining.

My daughter and I went to a mall with my two grandchildren, who were quite small. After making our purchases, we walked to the car, only to find the car locked and our keys missing. I volunteered to return to the store we were in last to retrieve the missing keys while she stayed with the children. Thinking that it was quite a long trek with the children, I was surprised at how quickly I was able to cover the distance alone. Suddenly, I felt the Spirit's gentle nudging as it occurred to me that this was what had happened in my own life.

I viewed my losses from another perspective. I had suffered many losses when my children were small. But the Lord had relocated me, supported me with good health care, and allowed me to finish my degree, reenter the workforce, and build my life spiritually, emotionally, and financially. When I reconnected with my children, I was able to support them at a time when it was most needed. Never would I have been able to cover so much ground so quickly with them in tow and a chronic condition to manage.

For many years, since I became licensed as a registered nurse at age twenty, I considered myself to have a job. I had dared to think beyond, wanting to specialize in some area, although the only road I had experience in was as a patient on a psychiatric unit. Employees with my history are rarely employed in that specialty.

I viewed from my limited perspective the many years I worked in long-term care as simply the only position I could find, as there was such a tremendous need for nurses in that area. But all along from a higher perspective, I was serving where I was called. I was listening to families and coworkers and handling staffing problems. I was dealing with long-term illnesses. I was working with patients who had experienced strokes and suffered from dementia. I was using critical-thinking skills and handling problems that were behavioral but often based on a medical condition. I was reading about mental illness, post-traumatic stress disorder, and bipolar disorder. I was journaling.

The word *wait* in scripture implies expectation.

To my utter surprise, I found upon opening the mailbox that the letter was addressed to *me*. The Lord was giving me a platform and a voice to be used for His purposes.

CHAPTER 17

SO YOU THINK YOU ARE A WRITER?

I BOUGHT A BRIEFCASE MANY YEARS BEFORE I needed one, although I did so for a reason. The long hours of tending at nursing homes had taught me that I needed to be grateful for my health and to nurture it. But the predicament of nurses nearing retirement had taught me another sad reality. Rarely was there a pension plan in place that would provide needed security in advanced age. Many nurses, including me, change positions frequently to prevent burnout. The briefcase represented a position beyond my limitations. I realized that such a position would use my unique, God-given talents and would compensate for my weaknesses.

This black briefcase was symbolic of the security I yearned for, the professionalism I craved, and the illness I had been forced to overcome.

I dared to pursue the study for the book that I knew was in me. I researched mental illness from many angles, never hitting on one explanation that satisfied my every question. It seemed to be a compilation of many factors, some of which were outside the control of the sufferer. I believed the goal was to bring them into control as much as possible.

I decided the best course of action would simply be to write *my* story. I knew there were many similarities with others battling a similar condition. I was not an authority on the subject. But I was an overcomer, by the grace of God.

I searched the internet for writing courses and writing clubs, never finding the time to get involved with either. Yet I knew I was meant to write my story in some capacity. I steered my life in that direction even if the vehicle I was driving was used, damaged, and badly in need of repairs.

I wrote my own story.

From my research into trauma, I learned that if the one suffering can give an actual dialogue to events that previously have not had a voice, it can be very helpful. The written account must be given to someone who is chosen carefully, someone who will not be wounded by the telling. There must be an awareness that the telling itself can be traumatic and needs to be balanced with the comforts of present reality. This was advice I eventually took to heart.

I did not recover the ordeal readily or easily. It was much like piecing together a jigsaw puzzle that had been blasted to smithereens. I learned that traumatic memory is stored in the brain differently than normal memory. The emotion often follows later, sometimes years later, in what is commonly called a flashback.[19]

---

[19] Bessel A van der Kolk,. Alexander C. McFarlane, and Lars Weisaeth, eds., *Traumatic Stress: The effects of Overwhelming Experience on Mind, Body, and Society* (New York: The Guilford Press, 1996), 279–302.

The flashback seems so real that in the words of my son returning from combat, "It feels like you are losing it."

I started with a brief summary that covered a two-year period, which took me days to write, one particular paragraph being the most painful to finally put on paper. After completing that struggle, I felt like a sponge wrung dry of poison. I stopped writing for a time and busied myself with work and activities I enjoyed, grounding myself in my new reality. Working through traumatic events is a process, not a one-time event. It was perhaps a couple of weeks later before I finally cried like a baby, mourning the losses I had never voiced but oh so keenly felt.

Next came the more difficult task of sharing it with someone. It seemed too ugly to communicate, yet I considered who might need to know. I also considered who I needed to tell, whether or not that person might want to know. We carry shame around until we tell the truth, often placing it where it belongs and thereby relieving us of the burden.

Eventually, I was able to write my entire story, neither embellishing it nor detracting from it. It was the story of triumph and failure, but it was also the story of triumph after failure.

Finding hope for the future, something that I had previously lost, I searched online for those with bipolar disorder who had gone on to live successful lives. I found that they were often artists, those who excelled in creative endeavors. I was, with that discovery, daring myself to be a writer.

I went on a retreat of sorts. I took a tent to a campground in the mountains with a few well-chosen books and a reading light. I remember the tears streaming down my face as I felt the Lord communicate, in no uncertain terms, on this matter.

Writing my story wasn't just a good idea; it was His idea. I had a few arguments as to why it was impossible: I did not have the educational achievement I meant to attain; I had never finished my bachelor's degree, let alone an advanced degree; shock therapy had shortened my attention span and made concentration more difficult; my financial resources were limited; I had no previous experience writing anything but letters or term papers; and my computer skills were nil. With all these thoughts swirling in my head, the story of Moses and the burning bush became clear. I was faced with one of two choices. Either I had heard God speak, telling me what to do, or I had not. And quite simply, if I was certain of the call, either I would go forward, or I would not.

This put all of my excuses in perspective. I moved forward. I simply needed a position that paid more and allowed me the needed time to write. Although I had applied at other nursing facilities from time to time, I had failed to overcome the obstacles. A nursing license that had once been on probation for a mental disorder was the highest hurdle; the interview was usually concluded as soon as the interviewer accessed her computer screen. I was not trying to hide that which would inevitably be discovered. I had met a physician who returned to work after a schizoaffective diagnosis. I recalled his witness of filling out over eighty applications before he finally found a position. His son spurred him on until he eventually succeeded.

After moving across the country, my first act of faith, I found another nursing position, but this position met my needs. Then I carved out a two-hour block of time three or four times a week and simply bandaged my bleeding soul with words. My prayer was that, in soothing my own soul, I might bandage another.

Although the end result was a mere 117 pages, I concluded it told the story simply, and in my nursing background, brevity in telling was always a plus.

I was absolutely clueless as to whom this manuscript would be sent or the process by which it would eventually be considered for publishing.

I had faith that was as infinitely small as a mustard seed, hope that was dim at best, and imperfect love that would strive and fail many times. I was cautiously optimistic that this combination might, incredibly, be enough for the task.

CHAPTER 18

THE HEAVENS WILL OPEN

THERE ARE CIRCUMSTANCES THAT SEEM irrevocable precisely because they have remained virtually unchanged for years. The analogy might be of a tree that yields but little fruit during a drought. To the onlooker, the situation might seem unalterable; the past would appear to predict the future. Yet all the while, the roots of God's sapling are growing deeper and deeper, just waiting for what might, impossibly, occur next.

The parched ground holds no pools of water. There is only sunbaked earth where once-flowing streams nourished the earth. The season of drought has been long, entirely too long, one might be tempted to think. Will the replenishing showers ever come?

How long shall we pray for rain? Are our pleas of desperation being heard? Do our cries, with hopes less than certain, touch heaven from earth?

How long, O God? How long shall we wait? The word *wait* implies expectancy, but my certainty lapses into fears of improbability when I am weak. Help me to hang on to your promises.

> There is an appointed time for everything. And
> there is a time for every event under heaven—
> A time to give birth and a time to die;
> A time to plant and a time to uproot what is
> planted.
> A time to kill and a time to heal;
> A time to tear down and a time to build up.
> A time to weep and a time to laugh;
> A time to mourn and a time to dance.
> A time to throw stones and a time to gather stones;
> A time to embrace and a time to shun embracing.
> A time to search and a time to give up as lost;
> A time to keep and a time to throw away.
> A time to tear apart and a time to sew together;
> A time to be silent and a time to speak.
> A time to love and a time to hate;
> A time for war and a time for peace.[20]

I have heard the experiences of joy and pain described as a pendulum. Exhilarating joy can follow excruciating pain, but the sway to the former can only occur after experiencing the same swing to the latter.

And so, we endure the pain. We swelter in the scorching heat, knowing that one day the naysayer will be proved wrong, and

---

[20] Ecclesiastes 3:1–8

at a precise, predetermined moment, the heavens will open. The accumulated mud will be washed. The Lord has heard.

The heavens *will* open. They have never really been closed, only silent.

God's shower of grace has not been denied, only held in reserve for His appointed hour.

CHAPTER 19

DISCOVERING MY HOME IS THE MANSION

I HAD OFTEN CONSIDERED MYSELF TO BE A failure, not necessarily on *any* path, but it was my heavenly Father who would bring His purposes to pass. I was to be the willing vessel.

I started viewing the crime scene of my life not so much as the result of my many sins, but instead as God's written record—written boldly with red ink—of one attempt to stand and survive. His purpose was that others might stand and survive. A poem that I read and reflected on during one of my hospitalizations gave me my first glimpse of what later became the hope that I clung to. It is called simply "The Weaving."

> My life is but a weaving
> Between my Lord and me:
> I cannot choose the colors
> He worketh steadily.

Oft time He weaveth sorrow,
And I, in foolish pride,
Forget He sees the upper
And I, the lower side.[21]

That He could use all the mess, all the untidy details, is still a wonder to me. But He not only uses the mess; He also turns the shame into a sharing with others so many souls might be saved. Thus, it is difficult to imagine a life more rewarding, more fulfilling than the very one He has given.

All of this occurs, by no means, in a short period of time. Yet my Lord is a sustainer who will carry His precious child through all the difficulty. He is "our refuge and strength, a very present help in trouble."[22]

I took a leap of faith; I moved across the country to reestablish myself in another community to which I felt I was being called. I would be closer to my adult children and their families. My original intent was to work in another nursing home, but through a series of events, I finally found the courage to apply at the local hospital. I interviewed for more than one unit, but the unit that was closest to my experience and dearest to my heart was a rehabilitation unit for brain injuries. I found myself dealing with behaviors that I was familiar with often, and I knew that I had finally found a home and a specialty.

I woke up one morning, early in my fifth decade, and realized that I was, after all, a registered nurse. Through lapses of illness, I had only been able at best to hope that I had achieved the goal I set

---

[21] Author unknown
[22] Psalm 46:1

early in life. Unable to advance in the traditional mode due to my inability to work extremely long hours and handle mountains of stress, I had finally found my unique niche. I had the opportunity to share with my patients not only my own experiences but also my faith.

One day shortly after I was hired, I saw an announcement posted in the elevator. A cardiologist at my hospital who had recently served overseas in the army was having a book signing in the lobby. His book, *A Doctor Looks at War*, was featured in the local newspaper, and I read every word with great interest. The publisher specialized in publishing first-time authors. I knew I was being pointed to the path for a long-ago promised book. All I needed was the courage to submit my manuscript and to risk the possibility that it would not be accepted.

But the Lord knew my heart's desire, that many would be helped through my testimony. It was my hopeful conclusion that my pain was not without purpose. I believed with growing confidence that I was meant to be the owner of the mansion!

CHAPTER 20

THE RETURN ADDRESS

DON'T THINK FOR A MOMENT THAT THIS abundant life—the joy and peace that come from relationship and purpose—is not a thing to be envied. While our ultimate foe is Satan, we struggle against those in his control. Jesus refers to this foe as the thief: "The thief comes only to steal and kill and destroy; I came that they may have life, and have *it* abundantly."[23]

If the thief is not after your dream, he can have impact on your mind, your body, your spirit, or your family.

But we are not left without a defense. Prayer, in the power of God's word, is the first line of defense. This preparation is outlined in Ephesians:

> Finally, be strong in the Lord and in the strength
> of His might. Put on the full armor of God, so that
> you will be able to stand firm against the schemes
> of the devil. For our struggle is not against flesh

---

[23] John 10:10

and blood, but against the rulers, against the powers, against the world forces of this darkness, against the spiritual *forces* of wickedness in the heavenly *places*. Therefore, take up the full armor of God, so that you will be able to resist in the evil day, and having done everything, to stand firm. Stand firm therefore, HAVING GIRDED YOUR LOINS WITH TRUTH, and HAVING PUT ON THE BREASTPLATE OF RIGHTEOUSNESS,

And having shod YOUR FEET WITH PREPARATION WITH THE GOSPEL OF PEACE; In addition to all, taking up the shield of faith with which you will be able to extinguish all the flaming arrows of the evil *one*.

And take THE HELMET OF SALVATION and the sword of the Spirit, which is the word of God. With all prayer and petition pray at all times in the Spirit, and with this, in view, be on the alert with all perseverance and petition for all the saints.[24]

This leads to the question of purpose. Just what is the purpose of an enemy? What are we to learn from those who betray, insult, rob, threaten, or seek to destroy us or those we love? First of all, we are to expect this. "Expect?" you might say. Yes, we are to expect to suffer in this world. If you question this fact, re-read Ephesians 6:12:

---

[24] Ephesians 6:10–18

> For our struggle is not against flesh and blood, but
> against the rulers, against the powers, against the
> world forces of this darkness, against the spiritual
> *forces* of wickedness in the heavenly *places*.

We suffer at the hands of those who have been blinded from the truth. And yet, it is our very response that is being critically weighed by our enemies. Thus, we may provide the very hope that is most sought by those who would injure us.

I pondered on the details of my dream once again. After I scaled the mud to finally retrieve the mail, I recalled the vivid detail of the lettering. The envelope was addressed to me! I recognized the style of the cursive writing from my past. It appeared as it now appears on a certificate awarded to me in high school. At the time, I was honored as a high achiever in music by a local university. I pondered on the respect of the moment from my past.

In contrast, and particularly puzzling to me, was the return address. I was not aware of it until I successfully assaulted the mud, the obstacle, to finally claim my inheritance. There were actually five names in the sender's space, but four of the names had been scrawled illegibly and had been lined through, apparently rendered void. In the middle, neatly printed, was the name of one I recognized. It was written simply, humbly, and beautifully.

As a nurse who deals with signatures every day, I am aware that a signature that cannot be read is an order that cannot be carried out. So the particular significance of an illegible signature is that orders will be rendered void. So I pondered the details of my life and thought back to those in authority over me who had no spiritual authority.

Only One who stood with spiritual authority had made me the recipient of riches undeserved yet promised to those who love the Lord.

CHAPTER 21

HE KNEW OF THIS PLAN ALL ALONG

I CAREFULLY CONSIDERED HOW TO PACKAGE my first manuscript before mailing it for consideration to the acquisitions team. I included a smiling picture from an obviously healthy lady and a brief note as to my intention to help others suffering with bipolar disorder. A few weeks after I mailed the text, I very sheepishly called the number I found online to follow up on my heart's desire.

"How long," I dared to ask "after a manuscript is received is the decision made as to whether or not it will be selected for publication?" My heart beat wildly in my chest as I spoke. When I received the reply from a courteous and friendly staff member, I thanked her and hung up.

I worked the evening shift on my unit, a rehab unit for brain injuries. The work was both challenging and rewarding.

I returned home one night shortly before midnight to check the messages on my answering machine. A soft, kind voice brought me to a standstill. A lady's voice introduced herself and said, "I would like to send you a contract for your manuscript, but I would like to talk with you first."

My heart stopped. I replayed the message. With astonishment, I replayed the message several times. I continued to replay the message, analyzing the words from every conceivable angle. *She wants to send me a contract!* I thought. *She wants to talk to me before she sends me a contract,* I considered. *She wants to talk to me to determine if she should send me a contract,* I judged.

As it was too late to call back, I was forced to wait until morning to know the outcome, although I considered the third choice to be most likely. I tried to sleep. When I returned her call the following morning, how would I sound? Would I be the polished, accomplished writer she was looking for? Would I be the childish scrawler who had never done more than write desperate letters? Finally, I decided I would just be myself. Anything else would be a lie. And eventually I drifted off to sleep, content that I had solved the first dilemma.

I awakened with the sound of the doorbell. I donned my bathrobe and sleepily walked to my front door to discover no one present. But there on my front porch, delivered by the Federal Express driver, was an envelope, and the sender was my publisher. I was dumbfounded that it contained the very contract that had been spoken of the previous evening, which had been sent overnight, no less.

The possibilities loomed in front of me. I was full of immense gratitude, incredulous wonder, and awe. All of these emerged larger than the fears I would have to face.

I was ready and willing to face whatever lay ahead, as I was quite certain I was on the path long ago promised. There were hurdles, to be sure, in the process of having my story published, but just as surely as the obstacle appeared, needed help would also show up. I can honestly say that I never questioned whether I had made the right decision after that time. Although the time from signing the contract to the release date of the book was a little less than a year, an inevitable waiting time, I was so busy between work, family, and the book that I don't remember the time as being slow at all.

It seemed to me that I was caught up in something far greater and more wide reaching than I had ever dared to dream. A new door had opened, one I had never intended to open. Yet God's grace, in the form of bipolar disorder, had opened this door to a world of possibilities so far beyond my own imaginings that all I could do was marvel at His plan.

By the time the book was published, I had been certified as a brain injury specialist by the Brain Injury Association of America. I considered myself specialized in a field that allowed me to grow. None of this occurred with my careful plans that never went awry. In fact, when I look back, I find a few books where I had written my unfeasible dreams in the margins. The impossibilities had been realized, not as anything I had carefully planned, but through God's grace that had given enough light day by day. I had dared to have that microscopic particle of faith, which was enough to believe that my God is a God of the impossible. Then on a steady path through joy, pain, and sheer drudgery, I had lived with only enough illumination for the next step.

He knew of this plan all along.

CHAPTER 22

LOVING MY NEIGHBORS

WHILE I STILL HAVE NEIGHBORS ON MY former side of the street, I now have new neighbors I am increasingly more aware of. They do not live in the land of scarcity, for they have learned the secret of abundant living. It is a world of giving. They give to the church and to others out of their fullness. Sometimes they give from their leanness with complete confidence that their Father who sees can supply their resulting lack. They give with their wealth, time, and talents to those in need and sometimes to those with wants. They give with hearts of compassion. Their generosity is not offered grudgingly, but most joyfully, for they know their true inheritance is in a heavenly kingdom with mansions already prepared for them.

I once heard a description of heaven and hell as told to me by a patient struggling with mental illness. The story, as it was conveyed to him, was a description of the two choices we have on this earth. Hell was a table spread with sumptuous food surrounded by people who each had a spoon that was too long to bring it to their own mouths. Thus, unable to feed themselves, they were all starving. In contrast, heaven was the same table with the same food surrounded by a different group of people who also had spoons that were too long. What distinguished the place as heaven was that this group of people had learned to feed each other. They were, therefore, filled with both contentment and joy.

The great irony of giving from our own supply is that the giver always receives more than he or she gives. It may come in an unexpected manner, in a way not totally understood. The receiving comes in different forms of blessing: joy, peace, health, a faithful marriage, godly children, a good job, and sometimes, a tax refund. Often, it comes in a changed perspective, enlightenment on a dilemma, a word of wisdom, or a loving church community. The gift may come where you did not know you had a need, and yet the problem has been solved before it has materialized.

By giving of time and talents, the giver also receives more than given. I often reflect on the time I spent teaching Sunday school to preschoolers and the many lessons I learned. I remember one particular Sunday when we were studying Joshua and the battle of Jericho. We built a tower of blocks complete with a wall surrounding it. We then marched around the walls seven times. As I was leading my army, I suddenly became aware how difficult it must have been to be the leader receiving such instructions from God; it went against everything man considered logical. A formidable foe surrounded by an equally formidable wall, and both were to be conquered by a parade, blowing horns and a shout. What everyone must have been thinking! The battle was most certainly first in the mind of the leader. Would he obey, or would he falter? As we blew our horns and gave a shout, the walls fell—this time with a little help. I came away with a new appreciation for those in positions of leadership.

Another Sunday school lesson that was most meaningful was our reenactment of the returning prodigal son. One particularly rowdy and boisterous five-year-old had volunteered to be the prodigal son. Knowing that he had not previously heard the story or the outcome, I watched as he seemingly enjoyed his descent into breaking all the rules.

But I will always remember the look of utter bewilderment on his face when his return was greeted with wildly enthusiastic forgiveness, complete with royal apparel and a party to celebrate. I was most aware of my own return and that my reaction was neither unusual nor unanticipated by my Father.

But just as we must learn to give, it is equally important that we learn to receive. My new neighbors know how to receive, for receiving is an act of humility. Never are we meant to be completely self-sufficient. "It is not good for the man to be alone" outlines our intended dependence on others.[25]

Recently, I was in a restaurant when I noticed a couple from my church at another table. As they were leaving, they insisted on buying my meal. While I had enough to pay for my own meal, I did not deny them the joy of paying for mine as I saw the radiant look on the faces of the givers. It was simply an act of kindness and love. It was not necessary, but it was welcome. I have learned how to receive. Later in the same day, a need arose for the cash in my purse, and it would not have been available had I not first received.

Never in this life will I be deserving of all my blessings. But I have learned how graciously and lavishly my Father loves to bless.

---

[25] Genesis 2:18a

CHAPTER 23

BIDDING OTHERS TO CROSS THE STREET

IT IS NOT ENOUGH TO SURVIVE YOUR OWN ordeal. We are delivered from our trials so we might help another find the passageway to freedom. No longer are we tagged with a diagnosis, although we may carry the burden of one. As a child of God, our new title is *servant*, and our new label might best be described as *survivor*. Better yet, our new ticket might be stamped *overcomer*.

Survivors have many strengths. To truly love oneself, these strong points must be used.

First, and most apparent, survivors have prevailed where others have not. Something within them, a spark yet to be fanned into a full flame has flickered but never gone out. A divine touch of providence not fully understood has allowed them to escape the box they were confined to. It is that same touch that has given them wings to soar to a future not previously imagined.

Living to tell the tale takes many forms. It can simply be

staying alive to piece together the details later. It may mean keeping your family together or putting them back together. The challenge may be finding the right medication to return to work. Or you may face living through the grief of losing a loved one. It may mean all of the above and then some. The light of God's word gives us new causes born of old pains.

Survivors often have a dedication to a cause that others may not understand as they cannot fathom the fervency behind such devotion.

When all of one's potency is used in the pursuit of a God-given goal, such an individual may see results far beyond what others can envision. Whereas at one time one may have been struck by lightning, it is the same bolt of energy that can now be harnessed for humankind's good. What light! What force! What electrifying experiences are possible!

Although we wish it wasn't so, one thing is certain: survivors and overcomers can only be created through suffering.

It is not easy to recruit others to suffer; it is far easier to find one who has endured suffering not anticipated or sought. So how should we go about recruiting others to our cause? The answer, quite simply, is to find another sufferer. Better yet, inspire another victim to *be* one such overcomer.

To give another who is trapped in a tunnel of despair one glimmer of light at the end of the tunnel is a gift beyond measure. Ideally, we have enough light that we can see the next step. But sometimes the night is so dark that we are uncertain if we have feet, let alone light. In those times, we desperately need human contact to inspire the faith we thought we had and to prove God's love that we shamefully may have questioned.

A survivor who has trudged the road ahead of you is in the best position to point the way, however grueling it may appear. Thus, we who are wounded warriors become once-broken healers.

I would challenge one with severe mental illness to find quality, compassionate, and competent help. Do it for the people you love, and one of those you most love should be yourself. God's command to love yourself first appears in the Old Testament:

> You shall not take vengeance, nor bear any grudge
> against the sons of your people, but you shall love
> your neighbor as yourself; I am the LORD.[26]

Jesus restated the command four times in the New Testament.[27] You are worthy of God's love as well as human love and respect.

Seek help for the hope of a better life, for the rewards of this one, and for the generations after you. Stay with it until the task is finished. Listen to the words you least want to hear. Apply the lessons you would rather ignore. Pay the dues, the fees, the respect you would rather not pay.

And sometimes, walk away from the relationships that keep you bound. Establish the relationships that lead to wholeness.

Finally, hold your head high. You have the courage to confront the unpleasant and the unwelcome. Do so as your assignment in life. And all the while, most of all, watch what God can do.

---

[26] Leviticus 19:18
[27] Matthew 19:19; Matthew 22:39; Mark 12:31; John 15:9

CHAPTER 24

SOUL SEARCHING

THERE WAS A TIME WHEN I DID A GREAT deal of soul searching on my journey to wholeness. Once I was attempting to mow my yard on my only day off. At the time, I held two jobs to make a house payment, and I was determined not to let my nicely landscaped investment become anything less. I kept trying to start my mower. I pulled the cord again and again. My frustration would end in yet another attempt to pull the cord, not knowing that divine intervention would be sent to rescue me from myself. I have only encountered a still, small voice a few times in my life. This was not the negative, accusing voice of mental illness. The voice wasn't audible and yet so certainly from Him that I've never doubted His Spirit's moving.

He simply, very quietly spoke into my hearing, "I never intended for you to work like a man."

I broke down in tears, amazed that He truly is the God who sees. Who would have thought He would speak to me over such a trivial matter? Yet the words were anything but trivial. They summed up what had been wrong up to that point. I left the mower in the yard, asked a friend to take it in for repairs, and took a much-needed nap.

Over the next few years, I became softer. I became more accepting of the cared-for femininity that I had tossed away while pursuing solutions to moving past mental illness and financing the needs of my family. I finally allowed the floodgates of grief that held back so much to finally open. I grieved over a child, a wife, and a mother. I grieved over me.

I contemplated my many dreams of an unidentified man. I was born into a culture and an age where women had distinct roles and to step outside of those boundaries would bring disapproval, or more likely, condemnation. Yet when my female identity had been destroyed, it was this male who came to the rescue. I found that he could be, if needed, aggressive, boldly direct, financially savvy, and ambitious. These traits are not unique to men; however, they were only assigned to men in the world I came from. A woman who manifested any of these behaviors, I was subconsciously taught, would not attract a man. Thus, she would likely remain childless and alone.

This unidentified one seemed to take on different roles, each of which benefited me. Once He was the soldier who carried me, wounded and weary, across the battlefield until He could find rest and provision for me. Then He was the Father who led me in a dance, having me stand back so He might admire my attire as I joyfully announced, "It is all one piece." And finally, He was the brother I kept looking for in the crowd as I dared to move closer to the front of a social gathering. To my delight, I discovered my brother to be the main speaker, who made sure that I was seated and attired with a bracelet identifying me as a brain injury patient. Joyfully, He announced, "I'll take care of you."

I find this man in scripture, this same one who displays attributes of protectiveness, provision, and security. I find Him in Psalm 45, where He is the King:

> Gird Your sword on Your thigh, O Mighty One,
> In Your splendor and Your Majesty!
> And in Your majesty ride on victoriously,
> For the cause of truth and meekness and righteousness;
> Let Your right hand teach You awesome things.
> Your arrows are sharp; The peoples fall under You;
> Your arrows are in the heart of the King's enemies.
> Your throne, O God, is forever and ever;
> A scepter of uprightness is the scepter of Your kingdom.
> You have loved righteousness and hated wickedness;
> Therefore God, Your God, has anointed You
> With the oil of joy above Your fellows. [28]

I find Him in Psalm 23, where He is the tender shepherd:

> The Lord is my shepherd, I shall not want.
> He makes me lie down in green pastures;
> He leads me beside the quiet waters.
> He restores my soul;
> He guides me in the paths of righteousness

---

[28] Psalm 45:3–7

For His name's sake.

Even though I walk through the valley of the shadow of death,

I fear no evil, for You are with me;

Your rod and Your staff, they comfort me.

You prepare a table before me in the presence of my enemies;

You have anointed my head with oil;

My cup overflows.

Surely goodness and lovingkindness will follow me all the days of my life,

And I will dwell in the house of the Lord forever.[29]

Ultimately, I find this man, who is also the Son of God, dying on the cross for my sins so I might be set free. What can be said after such a humbling display of love? Can I deny that such a One will always be there for me?

After moving to a military community, and shortly before I took my current position working with brain injuries, I joined a United Methodist Church near my home—the church God led me to join. I developed a close friendship with a retired nurse who had worked as a psychiatric nurse at the Veteran's Administration. I heard her speak of her career treating victims of mental illness and combat stress. She listened to me as I spoke of my struggles as I started a new position in a new community. She inspired me with her life and the many contributions she had made not only to war casualties but also to her family and community.

Eventually she encouraged me as a writer, proofreading the

---

[29] Psalm 23:1–6

final edit of my first book. On the day the book was released, she sent me flowers and a card of best wishes that simply read, "Congratulations on your first book!" Later, upon another milestone, my first book signing, she sent me a second bouquet with another note that simply said, "Congratulations—looking forward to you next one. Love, Jean."

Well, I must say, I had never considered that I could write a "next one" until this dear lady seemed to make it an imperative. It was certainly cause for reflection. I had spent fifteen years and a lifetime of struggle producing the first one. But Jean would not give up. The notes were also followed by phone calls. When I was in the throes of euphoria, not mania, over the fact that anyone would actually read my story, Jean would gently bring me down to earth with words like, "Now would be a good time to start your next book." I knew I was being given direction from a godly lady, so I intended to comply. *But what*, I wondered, *would I write about?*

At one of my book signings, in a large, very busy store shortly before the holiday season, I meekly sat up my table. I was not quite certain how a book on bipolar illness would be received during a festive time, but I soon had my answer. I would reveal the subject matter and get a variety of responses, but it seemed the vast majority of people were touched by the subject. Eventually, I sold all of my books, but that is not what I remember most about the event.

One of the purchasers took a seat on the floor, just to be near my table. She was a teenager who revealed that her mother was bipolar, but she refused to seek any help. For two hours, this little girl poured out her heart.

"How can I make her get help?" she pleaded.

I was brought back to my own childhood, my own helplessness. I wanted to say, "You cannot force her to do anything, but you have to take care of you," but I would not have received such information at that age. I wasn't sure that she would. But I committed the situation to prayer, and I believed that I was given the next assignment.

CHAPTER 25

AND THE WINDS BLEW

And the rain fell, and the floods came, and the winds blew and slammed against that house; and *yet* it did not fall, for it had been founded on the rock. (Matthew 7:25)

WE ARE TO EXPECT STORMS IN THIS LIFE. With floodwaters swirling around us, we are meant to keep afloat.

The expression "paddle your own canoe" means to act independently and determine one's fate. I do not propose that we should each paddle our own canoe. A canoe is best propelled with at least two travelers, each with a paddle, one on each side. We were never meant to go it totally alone. God told Adam it was not good for him to be alone.[30] Of note is the fact that God had access to Adam while he was in the garden. And Adam had

---

[30] Genesis 2:18a

access to God.[31] Yet God was speaking of Adam's need for human companionship.

When we are faced with troubling emotions, it simply isn't wise or profitable to keep them all to ourselves. The very sharing gives legitimacy to that which may be denied. Sometimes emotions are based on present situations; sometimes they are based on past events that may have been triggered by seemingly benign occurrences.

Research on trauma and recovery from such began in earnest after the Vietnam War.[32]

There is little doubt that many of those suffering from mental illness have encountered trauma of some kind.[33] The abuse might have occurred in childhood, although not necessarily. More than likely inpatient psychiatric admissions and an overly crowded population of sufferers can cause traumatic memories that need healing. The medical system is forced to pigeonhole each individual into a specific diagnosis, labeling them as a disorder rather than an individual. This is damaging in itself.

To begin the work of recovery, one must be able to put a narrative to events that have transpired up to that point. I am reminded of a psychiatrist who asked me a simple question during an interview at the beginning of a state hospital commitment. It was approximately my twentieth inpatient stay, which occurred in one of five states.

She simply said, "And why are you here?"

I wanted to answer the question; I simply did not know where

---

[31] Genesis 3:8

[32] Judith Herman, *Trauma and Recovery: The aftermath of violence—from domestic abuse to political terror* (New York: Basic Books, 1997), 26–27.

[33] Ibid., 122–29.

to begin. How could I condense the narrative so that the full impact could be shared in the healthcare worker's allotted time? I remember staring at her and feeling helpless to do the question justice. As it was, I stared helplessly and said nothing.

Yet it is important to tell the story. Until we are believed by another, it is often impossible to feel the full impact ourselves. I would frequently imagine a patient was telling me, the nurse, my story. What would my judgment be of the situation in that case? Would I feel compassion for the teller, the same compassion that I was denying myself? What conclusions would I come to? What course of action would I consider wise?

I can choose the other person or persons in my canoe. Sometimes the other is a physician. Sometimes the other is a close friend with considerable insight. The individual can be a counselor, a mental health worker, a sister, a brother, or a mate. The other person cannot be an individual of lesser strength or a dependent child. Too often, those recovering from traumatic emotions turn to comfort alone and do not acknowledge the need for might. Others in our canoe need to be strong enough to respond to our inevitable times of weakness, just as we are willing to compensate for theirs.

Together, you can enjoy the stream of calm as you explore the roaring tributary that joined your brook at some point upstream. Together, you can keep the canoe from capsizing.

You really can't see anything unless you have an equal in your canoe.

CHAPTER 26

AN INHERITANCE

WHILE WE ARE PROMISED A HEAVENLY inheritance, there is also an earthly reward for our faith. The sad truth is that few are willing to go for it. The Old Testament account of God's people being led out of bondage in Egypt gives us needed insight into why.

While they were slaves in Egypt, the people suffered greatly. But God had answered their prayers and was giving them a great deliverance. The promised abundance, their inheritance, was described as a land flowing with milk and honey. This promised plenty was a great incentive to move forward. There were many miraculous deliverances from the sea that parted, allowing their escape to the manna that fell from heaven to feed them. Yet, the great majority failed to trust the protective hand of God leading their way. This negative mindset was so entrenched that upon spying out the Promised Land and acknowledging the mindboggling abundance, only two members of the scouting party were willing to face the so-called giants that awaited them.

In the end, only these two, Joshua and Caleb, were rewarded with the promised land of plenty. The others who reached this inheritance were the children, the next generation that followed the faithless one.

I am reminded of an exercise given to me by my church when I was still in the abyss of failure and need. I was told to put on paper each prayer request and how it had been answered. This exercise, dutifully carried out, revealed to me my innate selfishness and just how much I took for granted, for I became aware of how faithful my Lord is. He is a God of the biggest problem and the smallest detail. I became aware that while I was always looking for an answer *my* way, He would graciously respond His way, which was infinitely better than my original request. His no was on a much higher plane than my yes would have been from my very limited and all-too-human perspective. Only in hindsight was I able to see this.

Some questions will never be answered on this side of heaven, but I have learned to trust.

I began to pray more effectively. My morose pessimism began to lift, replaced with the firm optimism of the certainty that I was in God's protective hand. I believe this is what happened in the lives of those who finally reached the Promised Land.

A second reason, besides lack of faith, kept others from enjoying an earthly reward. Every blessing is a burden. I have often reflected on these words since I first heard them spoken in a sermon. Nothing more clearly demonstrates this than Caleb's inheritance. Rewarded for his faithfulness, he is in his eighties when he is finally given what he has requested and long waited for. Caleb gets a mountain. This is not Mt. Rainier National Park in all its peacefulness with paved roads, lodges, and park rangers. Caleb gets a rugged mountain, warfare, and what I can only imagine required a great deal of toil to manage. But all the work aside, Caleb had milk and honey, and most likely, a great view.

Onlookers may have envied Caleb's stronghold and his view. But the path of faithfulness is not a stroll in the park—a leisurely stroll will not get you to the summit. Burdens faithfully carried become larger burdens faithfully carried until the faith muscles are able to make the climb.

Not everyone wants to work as hard as Caleb.

My favorite scriptural example of finally finding God's abundance is beautifully portrayed in the story of Ruth. A Moabite, she married into a Jewish family living in Moab. The family suffered great tragedy as all the men died.

A young widow, she makes the heroic decision to return with her mother-in-law to Israel, even though she is warned that there is no promise of a future for her; she is a member of a disdained race. She will forever be a foreigner. Yet she is so inspired by the God of her mother-in-law that she is loyal to this woman first and foremost. She humbles herself to the poverty program of Israel; she gleans in a field. It is her work ethic that attracts the attention of the onlookers, particularly Boaz, who is the owner of the field. She does not know that this man is a kinsman of her mother-in-law and has the legal right to "redeem" her. But it is her mother-in-law who puts a plan in action, giving Ruth directions that she faithfully carries out despite the risks. In the end, Ruth has a new life, a new husband, and a child.

Not everyone wants to be humbled to foreigner status or work in the poverty program.

What are you being asked to do that you are unwilling to do? Build your faith muscles and reconsider.

CHAPTER 27

EXPECT THE GOOD

"IN EVERYTHING GIVE THANKS; FOR THIS IS God's will for you in Christ Jesus."[34]

I now expect the good, although it was not always so. My mindset changed when I learned to operate with the above instructions. This was perhaps my most difficult act of obedience.

How can you give thanks for tragedy and heartbreak? This is often a litmus test that separates believers from Christ followers, for God is good. He is not somewhat good but wholly and perfectly good. In our humanness, we attribute our own sinful motives to His character. We overlook the human condition and the evil that has been loosed in this present age. We dodge responsibility for our own actions at every conceivable opportunity.

Might a more dreadful situation have been averted? Might He be answering the very prayer we prayed, giving us exactly what we asked for albeit in a manner we may not have wanted? And yet, might the eventual outcome be far above our little request

---

[34] 1 Thessalonians 5:18

and encompass myriads of souls we have not had the generosity to pray for?

Perhaps God's purposes might be a nation of people finally receiving an inheritance when I have only been concerned with my own. And yet, while I finally become aware of His generosity in the face of my selfishness, I am humbly aware that He has attended to every detail of my homecoming. All that I need or will ever need has been prepared.

My mansion stands ready. The red carpet has been rolled out, every light is on, and the table has been magnanimously prepared, in the presence of my enemies, no less.

While I work diligently toward the purposes the Lord reveals for my life, I am not a workaholic. My life has fullness, roundness, and wholeness. I walk with my Shepherd, and He gently tends every lamb in His flock. I do not look back on my failures, as the past is the past. I am not the person who failed but the one who emerged from the failure. It is my hope to pass the gift of another chance to any who would have it.

For God is good, and we are to expect His goodness.

ABOUT THE AUTHOR

Have your dreams been dashed upon the rocks with every new wave of life? Was your voice drowned long ago in a sea of woe?

Have you lost hope of recovering your life? Have you lost the courage to take back your voice and make your dreams a reality? In this true story of growth, Rose Anne takes you from a place of hopelessness and despair to a world full of expectation and blessings. Join Rose Anne as she writes, from her own experience, of finding the courage to approach *The Mansion Across the Street*.

Rose Anne Daniels is the pen name of a grandmother in Arkansas. Having recovered from tragic loss due to gravely disabling bipolar disorder, she spent eleven years working on a rehabilitation unit for brain injuries. Rose Anne has been a registered nurse for over forty years. She continues to write and to work as a rehabilitation nurse. Rose enjoys a full life with family and friends.